crochet
PINK

26 Patterns to Crochet for
Comfort, Gratitude, and Charity

JANET REHFELDT

Martingale®
Create with Confidence

Crochet Pink: 26 Patterns to Crochet for Comfort, Gratitude, and Charity
© 2013 by Janet Rehfeldt

Martingale®
19021 120th Ave. NE, Ste. 102
Bothell, WA 98011-9511 USA
ShopMartingale.com

Printed in China
18 17 16 15 14 13   8 7 6 5 4 3 2 1

Library of Congress Cataloging-in-Publication Data is available upon request.

ISBN: 978-1-60468-353-0

Mission Statement

Dedicated to providing quality products and service to inspire creativity.

CREDITS

President and CEO: Tom Wierzbicki
Editor in Chief: Mary V. Green
Design Director: Paula Schlosser
Managing Editor: Karen Costello Soltys
Acquisitions Editor: Karen M. Burns
Technical Editor: Ursula Reikes
Copy Editor: Sheila Chapman Ryan
Production Manager: Regina Girard
Cover Designer: Adrienne Smitke
Interior Designer: Adrienne Smitke and Connor Chin
Photographer: Brent Kane
Illustrators: Cheryl Fall and Kathryn Conway

Contents

I am not cancer. Cancer is not my name. Cancer is the disease I have. I wear the ribbon of hope at fundraisers, walkathons, that type of thing. But I don't want to wear it every day. I'm a person, not a cause. A collection of designs that use the color pink but not the ribbon is a wonderful idea. Not only because the crocheted items are beautiful, but also because they're designed for comfort, not designed as a badge or proclamation.

> *~via Pat S. and an anonymous friend*

Introduction

According to NationalBreastCancer.org and Komen.org, it's estimated that each year, over 220,000 women in the United States will be diagnosed with breast cancer and more than 40,000 will die from the disease. Breast cancer is the leading type of cancer and cause of cancer deaths in women worldwide. Few people haven't, in some way, been touched by this disease. If we haven't been diagnosed ourselves, we have a family member or friend who has.

Pink is the designated color of hope for breast-cancer awareness. This book was created with this in mind. I wanted to create designs using exotic and feel-good-next-to-your-skin yarns such as alpaca, silk, cashmere, superfine merino, silk-and-merino blends, silk-and-alpaca blends, and organic cotton. For those wanting to use something other than the listed yarn, I've included a guide to exchanging yarns in the "Getting Started" section (page 6).

I used a lot of variety when selecting shades of pink for this book. The colors range from the palest of pale to the brightest and deepest of roses and fuchsias. I've used solids, tonals, hand-painted, and variegated yarns, sometimes bringing in other shades or colors to accentuate the pinks. In recognition of other types of cancer, I've included a list of "Cancer Awareness Colors" (page 92) so that you can choose to crochet any of these designs in a different color.

I hope these designs inspire you, and I hope they provide comfort to you and/or a loved one, friend, or caregiver in your life. I wish you peace and good health.

~Janet

Getting Started

This section will help you with lots of little tips and suggestions on yarns, yarn substitution, gauge, tools, and special stitches.

YARNS

I used lots of exotic and luxury yarns such as cashmere, silk, and alpaca for the designs in this book. They are soft, cozy, and feel wonderful—not only to wear, but also while crocheting with them. Be sure to read the labels for fiber content and care.

SUBSTITUTING A DIFFERENT YARN

If you choose to substitute a different yarn for a project, here's how to determine the right yarn size and number of skeins you need. Each project has a list of materials, including the yarn used, and next to the yarn is an icon that looks like a skein of yarn with a number in the middle. This tells you the yarn weight (or size) to look for when you shop for a substitute. Many yarn labels include this icon so you can easily find yarn that's the same weight.

Yarns of similar weight and texture usually interchange well. Use a yarn that's in the same weight (or size) category that the pattern calls for, such as sport weight or worsted weight. However, due to the type of fiber, number of strands (or plies), and how tightly it was spun, there can be a large difference in the number of yards between skeins of two different yarns of the same weight.

First, take a look at the materials listed in your pattern. The number of skeins required for the project, multiplied by the number of yards (or meters) listed per skein, equals the total number of yards needed to complete your project. Divide the number of yards listed in the pattern by the number of yards in one skein of the substitute yarn to calculate the number of skeins needed of substitute yarn.

For example, if four skeins of the required yarn have 125 yards each, the total number of yards needed to complete the project is 500 yards: 4 skeins x 125 yards per skein = 500 yards. If the substitute yarn has 130 yards per skein, then you'll need four skeins: 500 total yards ÷ 130 yards = 3.84 skeins (round up to four).

> **Shopping Tip**
>
> Most cell phones have a calculator, so when you're out shopping for your yarn you can easily calculate the amount of yarn you need.

SPIFFY TOOLS

An assortment of tools for crochet.

It rarely takes special tools to crochet your projects. The right yarn, the right hook, and you're ready to begin. However, there are some great tools and gadgets that can be helpful and fun to use.

- **Hooks.** There are some amazingly beautiful crochet hooks available. However, hooks may vary in size from one manufacturer to the next. For example, a G hook may be 4.00 mm from one manufacturer and 4.25 mm from a different manufacturer. The hook sizes listed in this book include both US and metric sizes, like this: H-8 (5 mm). If your hook doesn't list millimeters, a needle/hook gauge, available at your local yarn shop, can help you determine the correct hook size.

- **Stitch markers.** Stitch markers are helpful in marking increases, decreases, and the beginning of rounds (see "Working with Markers" on page 8). Locking stitch markers or knitter's pins can be very useful. There's no coil to catch in your yarn like a safety pin can often do, and the markers tend to stay where you put them (marking corners on shawls, for example, or keeping a loop from unraveling when putting down a project), whereas split-ring markers can fall out.

- **Row counters.** Row counters are handy for tracking the rows on stitch-pattern repeats and the number of times you need to increase or decrease in a pattern.

- **Tape measures.** A tape measure is a must for taking accurate measurements and checking your gauge.

- **Needles.** Large, blunt-end tapestry needles are necessary for weaving in ends and sewing seams (see "Finishing" on page 10).

- **Pins.** Long, straight pins with large heads are perfect for pinning pieces in place while blocking them (see "Blocking" on page 11).

- **Blocking wires.** Blocking wires are especially handy for blocking large pieces, such as shawls, shrugs, and other garments (see "Blocking" on page 11).

- **Scissors.** Scissors are a necessity for snipping yarn ends. They work much better than breaking off your yarn.

SPECIAL INSTRUCTIONS AND STITCHES

In this section you'll learn more about crochet techniques, such as gauge, adding a new yarn, and working with markers, as well as detailed how-to instructions for a variety of stitches.

Calculating Your Gauge

Because of the wonderful and exotic types of yarns used to make the projects in this book, we tried to make the most of every last bit of fiber. Many of the patterns use most, or almost, all of the yarn listed. To make sure your project matches the measurements given in the pattern, and that you have enough yarn to complete your project, take time to make a gauge swatch.

Make a chain of 24 stitches; work 20 rows in the stitch pattern listed in the gauge. Measure the width of the swatch in several places. Divide the 24 stitches by your width measurement to get the number of stitches per inch. Measure the length of the swatch. Divide the 20 rows by your length measurement for the number of rows per inch.

If you have more stitches per inch than the required gauge, try a larger hook. If you have fewer stitches per inch, try a smaller hook. If your stitches match but your rows are slightly off, it's usually a matter of correcting your tension. If you have fewer rows than listed in the pattern, tighten up your tension. If you have more rows, loosen up a bit.

Working into the Bottom of a Chain

Working into the bottom loop (or hump) of the beginning chain creates a smooth and clean edge. Not only will the beginning edge match the ending (or top edge), sometimes making it so you don't have to edge your work, but it also makes it easier to work into later on if you are adding edging or finishing.

Working in the Loops of Stitches

Normally you'll be instructed to work into both loops of a stitch; however, some instructions will have you work into just the front or the back loop to create a different look or texture.

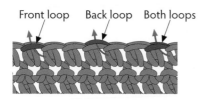

Front loop   Back loop   Both loops

Adding New Yarn

Where and how you join new yarn can impact the look of your project. I use one of the following two methods, depending on the type of project.

Method 1. When adding new yarn, try to do it at the end or beginning of a row or round if possible. This way if an end starts to work itself free, it's less noticeable. Work the last two loops of the stitch off the hook with the new strand of yarn, leaving 6" to 8" tails on both the old and new yarn strands for weaving in.

Method 2. When working with large projects, a Russian join is very useful since you can work it anywhere in the row or round. If the yarn is plied, run the tail through the plies; if the yarn is unplied (called a single), run the tail through the fibers of the yarn.

Thread one of your yarn ends on a yarn needle and insert the needle into the ball-end strand of yarn, drawing it through about 2" inside the plies. Pull the needle and yarn tail through the strand of yarn, leaving a small loop at the end. Slip the other strand of yarn into the small loop.

Repeat with the second strand, passing the needle through this strand as you did the first strand. Tug on the yarn ends to tighten the loops. Trim the remaining excess yarn.

Working with Markers

The pattern instructions will tell you to place a marker (PM) in a specific stitch or area. This marks the beginning of a row or round or marks increases or decreases. For increasing and decreasing, you'll be instructed to work up to a specific number of stitches prior to or at the marker. Here's an example: "sc to 3 sts prior to marker." Locate the marker and count back three stitches, excluding the stitch with the marker. Then work as stated in the directions.

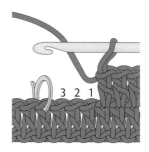

SPECIAL CROCHET STITCHES

The projects in this book are written assuming you have a basic knowledge of crochet. Instructions for special stitches and techniques are explained below. If you need information on more basic stitches, such as chaining, slip stitch, single crochet, or double crochet, you can find information at ShopMartingale.com/HowtoCrochet.

Extended Single Crochet (esc)

Insert hook into next st, YO, pull yarn through, YO, pull through 1 lp on hook, YO, pull through 2 lps on hook.

Double Crochet Foundation (dcf)

By starting your work with the double crochet foundation, you end up with an edge that's more elastic than an edge started with a traditional ch. Ch 3, YO, insert hook into third ch from hook through fl and bottom hump of ch. YO, pull yarn through st.

YO, pull yarn through 1 lp on hook (ch 1 made).

YO, pull yarn through 2 lps on hook.

YO, pull yarn through last 2 lps on hook (first dc made). *YO, insert hook through fl and bottom hump of ch, YO, pull yarn through, ch 1, YO, pull yarn through 2 lps on hook, YO, pull yarn through last 2 lps on hook*, rep from * to *, making each new dc in the previous ch.

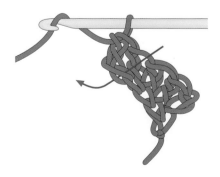

Half Double Crochet Foundation (hdcf)

Work the same as the double crochet foundation st through making the ch 1 (as shown in double crochet foundation), then YO, pull through all 3 lps on hook as for a normal half double crochet stitch.

Crossed Stitches

Crossed stitches are worked by skipping a st, working into the next st, then working into the st that was skipped (example shows double crochet). Some crossed sts may have you sk a st, work a dc in the next st, then a ch st, then work a double crochet in the skipped st.

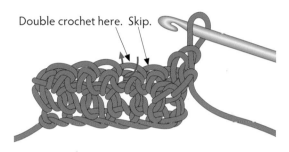

Front-Post Double Crochet (FPdc) and Back-Post Double Crochet (BPdc)

For front-post sts, YO, insert hook from front to back around indicated st post, YO, pull yarn through, (YO, pull yarn through 2 lps) 2 times. Always sk st in back of FPdc unless otherwise directed.

For back-post sts, YO, insert hook from back to front around indicated st, YO, pull yarn through, (YO, pull yarn through 2 lps) 2 times. Always sk st in back of BPdc unless otherwise directed.

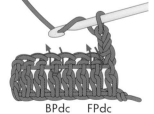

BPdc   FPdc

Front-Post Treble Crochet (FPtr) and Back-Post Treble Crochet (BPtr)

These sts are worked the same as front- and back-post double crochets, except you YO twice before inserting the hook around the post of the indicated st, then (YO and pull through 2 lps) 3 times. Always sk st in back of FPtr or BPtr unless otherwise directed.

INCREASING AND DECREASING (INC AND DEC)

When increasing, work two stitches into one stitch. When decreasing, work over two stitches.

Single Crochet Decrease (sc2tog)

Insert hook into next st, YO, pull yarn through st, insert hook into next st, YO, pull yarn through st, YO, pull yarn through all lps on hook.

Extended Single Crochet Decrease (esc2tog)

(Insert hook into next stitch, YO, pull lp through) twice, 3 lps on hook, YO, pull through 1 lp on hook, YO, pull through 2 lps on hook.

Half Double Crochet Decrease (hdc2tog)

YO, insert hook into next st, YO, pull yarn through st, insert hook into next st, YO, pull yarn through st, YO, pull yarn through all lps on hook.

Double Crochet Decrease (dc2tog)

YO, insert hook into next st, YO, pull yarn through st, YO, pull yarn through 2 lps, YO, insert hook into next st, YO, pull yarn through st, YO, pull yarn through 2 lps, YO, pull yarn through all lps on hook.

Slip Stitch Decrease (slst2tog)

Insert hook into next st, YO, pull yarn through st, insert hook into next st, YO, pull yarn through all lps on hook.

FINISHING

In this section you'll learn how to create an invisible seam and block your finished projects.

Invisible Seaming

There are slightly different methods for seaming, depending on the area to seam.

For cuffs or bands. Align the edges with the right sides facing out. With a large blunt tapestry needle and matching yarn, insert the needle under the front loop on one side edge of the piece, and then under the back loop on the opposite side edge of the piece. Pull the needle and yarn through. Continue in this manner along the edge to be sewn.

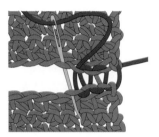

For mitten tops, toes, and heels. With the right sides of the piece facing out, align the stitches on each piece. With a large blunt needle and matching yarn, insert the needle under the post between two stitches and pull the needle through. Insert the needle under the post between two stitches on the opposite side and pull the needle through. Work from one side of the piece to the other side of the piece. Pull the thread up every three or four stitches to close the stitched portion. Continue in this manner along the edge to be sewn.

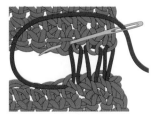

For side seams. With the right sides facing you, align the rows of your work, keeping the pieces smooth and even. With a large blunt needle and matching yarn, begin at the bottom edge of the right piece. Insert the needle under the post and pull the needle through; then on the left piece, insert the needle under the post of the corresponding row and pull the needle through. Insert the needle into the same space you came out on the right piece, going under the post of the next row. Insert the needle into the same space you came out on the left piece, going under a post of the next row. Work from one side to the other, pulling the thread up after every three or four stitches to close that portion of the seam. Do not pull so tight that you gather the seam. Your edges should be smooth and even.

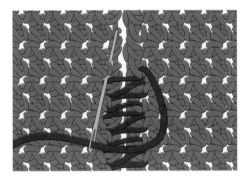

Blocking

Blocking is used for shaping each piece to the finished measurements given for your project. It also opens the stitch structure, shapes edgings, and realigns any stitches or rows that may have skewed while you were crocheting.

Steaming. Make sure you've read the care instructions on the yarn label. Steaming works well for wool, silk, and cotton, but not so well for acrylics, acrylic blends, and blends containing a lot of nylon. If you oversteam acrylics and some superwash wools, they'll wimp out, never to be recovered—no matter how many times you wash them. Likewise, yarns containing nylon can become hard and crunchy with oversteaming.

Pin your piece out to the measurements given in your pattern. Make sure to protect the surface with towels or padding. Hold the iron at least 6" above your crocheted piece and lightly steam it. Allow the piece to dry.

Misting. Use a spritzing or misting bottle, available at drug stores or hardware stores, and fill with cool, plain water. Once you've pinned your project to the listed measurements, lightly spritz with water and allow to dry. In some cases you may find that lightly spritzing first, and then pinning, can be easier, especially when blocking cotton and linen.

Wet blocking. In this method you'll saturate your project. Make sure you've read the care instructions to be sure your fiber can be fully saturated with water. There are several fiber-safe washes, soaks, and rinses on the market to use when wet blocking. Immerse your project in cool water in a sink or bathtub. Allow the garment or project to soak until fully wet, or as instructed for the product you're using, but do not agitate the piece. Gently squeeze out the water and roll the item in towels, squeezing as much excess water out as possible without wringing or twisting it. Then smooth the piece onto a padded flat surface (I normally use layers of heavy towels on a spare bed), smoothing the item from the center outward, until it reaches the finished measurements. You may need to use a few heavy pins where needed. Allow your project to air dry. This may take several days. You can shorten drying time by placing a nonheated fan near the area.

Blocking boards and blocking wires. You can purchase pliable, interlocking blocking boards in yarn shops or online that work great. I don't advise using steam with these; some may melt. Misting or wet blocking may be the wiser choice with these types of blocking boards.

Blocking wires normally come in sets of different lengths and may or may not include heavy T-pins (pins with a flat head shaped like a T). Insert the wires along the side, top, and bottom edges of the item, and then pin the wires out to the listed measurements. On shawls with points, insert wires through the tips of the points to shape them. You can then steam or spritz and allow to dry.

Ripples and Lace Stole

A touch of mohair gives this beautiful lace ripple stole a loft and aura that wraps you in luxurious style. Shades of pink and rose blend with taupe and charcoal, bringing to mind wild roses. Close your eyes, wrap yourself up, and imagine a peaceful garden.

By Janet Rehfeldt

SKILL LEVEL: Intermediate

FINISHED DIMENSIONS:
26" x 68" from peak to peak (after blocking)

FEATURED STITCHES

Chain (ch)

Half double crochet foundation (hdcf); page 9

Half double crochet (hdc)

Slip stitch (sl st)

MATERIALS

3 skeins of Lace from Patons (80% acrylic, 10% mohair, 10% wool; 3 oz/85 g; 498 yds/455 m) in color 1204 Woodrose

Size 7 (4.5 mm) crochet hook or sized needed for gauge

2 stitch markers

Tapestry needle

GAUGE

5¼ shells and 12 rows = 4" in patt

PATTERN NOTE

Begin each new skein in color sequence to keep integrity of color patterning in stole.

SPECIAL STITCH

Shell: (hdc, ch 2, hdc) in st or ch sp indicated.

STOLE

Row 1 (RS): Ch 3 (counts as first hdc), work 204 hdcf sts, turn—205 hdcf.

Row 2: Ch 1, hdc in first hdc, PM, sk next st, (hdc, ch 2, hdc) in next hdc, (sk next 2 sts, shell in next hdc) 4 times, *sk next 2 sts, work (shell, ch 3, shell) in next hdc, (sk next 2 sts, shell in next hdc) 4 times, sk next 2 sts, hdc in next hdc, sk next 3 sts, hdc in next hdc, (sk next 2 sts, shell in next hdc) 4 times; rep from * to last 20 sts, sk next 2 sts, (shell, ch 3, shell) in next hdc, (sk next 2 sts, shell in next hdc) 5 times, sk next st, tr in last hdc, turn.

Row 3: Ch 1, hdc in first tr, PM, hdc in ch-2 sp of next shell, work shell in each ch-2 sp of next 5 shells, *(shell, ch 3, shell) in next ch-3 sp; work shell in ch-2 sp of next 4 shells; hdc in next ch-2 sp, sk the 2 lone hdc, hdc in next ch-2 sp; work shell in ch-2 sp of next 4 shells; rep from * to last ch-3 sp, (shell, ch 3, shell) in ch-3 sp, shell in ch-2 sp of next 5 shells, hdc in next ch-2 sp, sk next hdc, tr in last hdc, turn.

Rep row 3 until piece measures 65" in length (relaxed) from peak to peak.

Next row: Ch 1, hdc in first tr, hdc in each hdc and in each ch-2 sp to first ch-3 sp, (hdc, dc, hdc) in ch-3 sp, *hdc in next hdc, hdc in next ch-2 sp, sk next hdc, rep from * to next ch-3 sp, (hdc, dc, hdc) in ch-3 sp, then rep from * to last 6 shells, working (hdc, dc, hdc) in each ch-3 sp, hdc in each hdc, hdc in each ch-2 sp, hdc in each of last 2 hdc, hdc in last tr.

Fasten off. Weave in ends. Block to finished measurements using method of choice (page 11).

Petals of Hope Shawl

Wrap yourself in the beauty and luxurious softness of merino and silk. The design is based on prayer shawls and uses chains and single crochets to create a petal-like effect. This shawl is worked in threes: three chains for each loop, three loops for each corner. For me, the three signify hope, love, and a cure.

By Rozetta Hahn
and Janet Rehfeldt

SKILL LEVEL: Experienced

FINISHED DIMENSIONS:
36" x 36" (after blocking)

FEATURED STITCHES

Chain (ch)

Double crochet (dc)

Single crochet (sc)

Slip stitch (sl st)

MATERIALS

1 skein of Findley from Juniper Moon Farm (50% merino, 50% silk; 3.5 oz/100 g; 798 yds/730 m) in color 11 Serendipity

Size H-8 (5 mm) crochet hook for shawl or size needed for gauge

Size F-5 (3.75 mm) crochet hook for border

5 stitch markers (4 of one color to mark corners; 1 different color for beg of rnd)

Tapestry needle

GAUGE

6 ch-3 lps and 8 ch-3 lp rnds = 4" with H hook when blocked

Gauge is important. You'll need all of the yarn in the skein. Place swatch or beg of shawl after 6 to 8 rnds on blocking wires or pin out to measure your gauge.

SHAWL

Shawl is worked from center outward with lace border

worked around outer edge once inner square is completed.

Do not ch 1 at beg of rnds and do not sl st rnds closed unless instructed. Make sure to keep beg of rnd and corner markers in place, moving them with each rnd.

Rnd 1: With H hook, ch 3, sl st in first ch to form circle, (ch 3, sc) in ring 4 times—4 ch-3 lps.

Rnd 2: Sl st into first ch-3 lp of rnd 1, *(ch 3, sc in ch-3 lp) twice; rep from * in each ch-3 lp around, PM in every other ch-3 lp to establish corners—8 ch-3 lps.

Rnd 3: (Ch 3, sc) in next ch-3 lp, PM for beg of rnds in ch-3 lp just made, *(ch 3, sc) 3 times in next ch-3 lp, PM in 2nd ch-3 lp to mark corner, (ch 3, sc) in next ch-3 lp; rep from * 3 times—16 ch-3 lps.

Rnd 4: *(Ch 3, sc) in each ch-3 lp to corner st, (ch 3, sc) 3 times, then sc once more in corner lp, PM in 2nd ch-3 lp to re-mark corner; rep from * 3 times, then (ch 3, sc) in rem ch-3 lps to end of rnd—24 lps.

Rnd 5: *(Ch 3, sc) in each ch-3 lp to corner st, ch 3, (sc, ch 3, sc) in corner ch-3 lp, PM in ch-3 lp to re-mark corner; rep from * 3 times, then (ch 3, sc) in rem ch-3 lps to end of rnd—28 ch-3 lps.

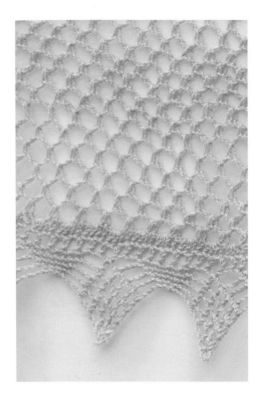

Rep rnds 4 and 5 until you have 58 lps per side, counting corner lps. Then rep rnd 5 once more. Sl st in first ch-3 lp on final rnd.

BORDER

Rnd 1: With F hook, ch 2 (counts as first dc), work 234 dc evenly spaced along each side, working 3 dc in each corner and PM in center dc to mark corner—936 total dc, counting 3-dc corners.

Rnd 2: Ch 3 (counts as first dc and ch 1), PM for beg of rnd, sk next dc, *(dc in next dc, ch 1, sk next dc) to corner, work (dc, ch 2, sk next dc) in corner, place corner marker in ch-2 sp; rep from * around. Sl st in top of beg ch 3, fasten off—117 ch sps from corner to st just before next corner and 468 total chs.

Rnd 3: Count back 6 ch-1 sps from corner ch-2 sp (do not count the corner ch 2 as one of the 6 sps) and attach yarn in dc just before 6th ch-1 sp. Sc in same st as join (this first st should be 13 sts prior to corner ch-1 sp), PM to indicate beg of rnd, [sc in next 8 sts, ch 4, sk 4 sts, (dc, ch 1, dc) in next ch-1 sp, ch 4, sk 4 sts] (first corner made), *sc in next 9 sts, ch 3, sk 4 sts, (dc ch 1, dc) in next ch-1 sp, ch 3, sk 4 sc, rep from * to 9 sts prior to corner ch-2 sp [sc in next 9 sts, ch 4, sk 4 sts, (dc, ch 1, dc) in next ch-1 sp, ch 4, sk 4 sc] (corner made), work from * 2 times more, then work from * to * to end of rnd, do not turn.

Rnd 4: [Sk first sc, sc in each of next 7 sc, ch 4, sk ch-4 sp, dc in next dc, (dc, ch 2, dc) in ch-2 sp, dc in next dc, sk next ch-4 sp] (corner made), *sk next sc, sc in each of next 7 sc, ch 3, sk ch-3 sp, dc in next dc, (dc, ch 2, dc) in ch-2 sp, dc in next dc*; (rep from * to * to 9 sc prior to next corner, work corner) 3 times; then rep from * to * to end of rnd, do not turn.

Rnd 5: [Sk first sc, sc in next 5 sc, ch 4, sk ch-4 sp, dc in each of next 2 dc, (dc, ch 2, dc) in ch-2 sp, dc in each of next 2 dc, sk next ch-4 sp] (corner made), *sk next sc, sc in next 5 sc, ch 3, sk ch-3 sp, dc in each of next 2 dc, (dc, ch 2, dc) in ch-2 sp, dc in each of next 2 dc*; (rep from * to * to 7 sts prior to next corner, work corner) 3 times, then rep from * to * to end of rnd, do not turn.

Rnd 6: [Sk first sc, sc in each of next 3 sc, ch 4, sk ch-4 sp, dc in each of next 3 dc, (dc, ch 2, dc) in ch-2 sp, dc in each of next 3 dc, sk next ch-4 sp] (corner made), *sk next sc, sc in each of next 3 sc, ch 3, sk ch-3 sp, dc in each of next 3 dc, (dc, ch 2, dc) in ch-2 sp, dc in each of next 3 dc*; (rep from * to * to 5 sts prior to next corner, work corner) 3 times, then rep from * to * to end of rnd.

Fasten off. Weave in ends. Block to finished measurements using method of choice (page 11).

> ⫸ *Faith, family, friends . . . three things in my life that keep me going and give me strength. Don't lose sight of these things. Keep your faith, family, and friends close. They are the mortar that keep the bricks of life together.*
>
> *~Anonymous*

Another Beautiful Sunrise Shawl

⋙ This warm shawl is crocheted from the bottom point, increasing toward the top edge using a shell stitch, and features a large shell grouping at the center back. Shades of pink, lavender, amber, and yellow bring to mind another beautiful sunrise.

By Janet Rehfeldt

SKILL LEVEL: Intermediate

FINISHED DIMENSIONS:
40" x 72" (after blocking)

FEATURED STITCHES

Chain (ch)

Double crochet (dc)

Single crochet (sc)

Slip stitch (sl st)

MATERIALS

6 skeins of Lanaloft Worsted from Brown Sheep Company, Inc. (100% wool; 3.5 oz/100 g; 160 yds/146 m) in color LL555W Saltwater Taffy

Size L-11 (8 mm) crochet hook or size needed for gauge

1 stitch marker

Tapestry needle

GAUGE

3¾ small groups and 7 rows = 4" in patt

SPECIAL STITCHES

Large group (lg-grp): 5 dc in ch-2 space

Small group (sm-grp): 3 dc in ch-2 space

SHAWL

Keep a marker in the center dc of lg-grp and move up with each row.

Row 1: Ch 4, dc in 3rd ch from hook (counts as first 2 dc), dc in last ch, turn—3 dc.

Row 2 (RS): Ch 1, sc in first dc, ch 1, (sc, ch 2, sc) in next dc, ch 1, sc in last dc, turn.

Row 3: Ch 4 (counts as first dc and ch 1), 5 dc in ch-2 sp, PM in center dc of lg-grp just made, ch 1, dc in last sc, turn—2 dc and 1 lg-grp.

Row 4: Ch 1 (2 sc, ch 2, 1 sc) in first dc (inc made), ch 2, (sc, ch 2, sc) in center dc of lg-grp, PM in ch-2 sp just made, ch 2, (1 sc, ch 2, 2 sc) in 3rd ch of beg ch 4, turn.

Row 5: Ch 3 (counts as first dc), 3 dc in next ch-2 sp, ch 2, sk 2 chs, 5 dc in next ch-2 sp, ch 2, sk 2 chs, 3 dc in next ch-2 sp, dc in last st, turn—2 sm-grps and 1 lg-grp.

Row 6: Ch 1, sc in first dc, *(sc, ch 2, sc) in next dc, sk 1 dc, (sc, ch 2, sc) in next dc (inc made)*, ch 2, sk 2 chs, (sc, ch 2, sc) in center dc of lg-grp, ch 2, sk 2 chs; work inc from * to * once, sc in top ch of beg ch 3, turn.

Row 7: Ch 3, *work sm-grp in each of next 2 ch-2 sps*, ch 2, sk 2 chs, work lg-grp in next ch-2 sp, ch 2, sk 2 chs; rep from * to *, dc in last st, turn—4 sm-grps and 1 lg-grp.

Row 8: Ch 1, sc in first dc, *(sc, ch 2, sc) in next dc, sk 1 dc, (sc, ch 2, sc) in next dc (inc made)*, (sc, ch 2, sc) in center dc of next sm-grp, ch 2, sk 2 chs, (sc, ch 2, sc) in center dc of lg-grp, ch 2, sk 2 chs, (sc, ch 2, sc) in center dc of next sm-grp; work inc from * to * once, sc in top ch of beg ch 3, turn.

Row 9: Ch 3, *work sm-grp in each of next 3 ch-2 sps*, ch 2, sk 2 chs, work lg-grp in next ch-2 sp, ch 2, sk 2 chs; rep from * to * once, dc in last st, turn—6 sm-grps and 1 lg-grp.

Row 10: Ch 1, sc in first dc, *(sc, ch 2, sc) in next dc, sk 1 dc, (sc, ch 2, sc) in next dc (inc made)*, (sc, ch 2, sc) in center dc in each of next 2 sm-grps, ch 2, sk 2 chs, (sc, ch 2, sc) in center dc of lg-grp, ch 2, sk 2 chs, (sc, ch 2, sc) in center dc in each of next 2 sm-grps; work inc from * to * once, sc in top ch of beg ch 3, turn.

Row 11: Ch 3, *work sm-grp in each of next 4 ch-2 sps*, ch 2, sk 2 chs, work lg-grp in next ch-2 sp, ch 2, sk 2 chs; rep from * to * once, dc in last st, turn—8 sm-grps and 1 lg-grp.

Row 12: Ch 1, sc in first dc, *(sc, ch 2, sc) in next dc, sk 1 dc, (sc, ch 2, sc) in next dc (inc made)*, (sc, ch 2, sc) in center dc of each sm-grp; ch 2, sk 2 chs, (sc, ch 2, sc) in center dc of lg-grp, ch 2, sk 2 chs, (sc, ch 2, sc) in center dc of each sm-grp to last sm-grp of row; work inc from * to * once, sc in top ch of beg ch 3, turn.

Row 13: Ch 3, work sm-grp in each ch-2 sp to center, ch 2, sk 2 chs, work lg-grp in next ch-2 sp, ch 2, sk 2 chs, work sm-grp in each ch-2 sp to last st, dc in last st, turn—10 sm-grps and 1 lg-grp.

Rep rows 12 and 13, working inc in first and last sm-grp on odd-numbered rows and adding 2 more sm-grps on even-numbered rows until there are 62 sm-grps with 1 lg-grp at center of shawl. Do not turn after last row.

EDGING

Working along side edge, *(sc, ch 2, sc) into side of each dc row and each sc row* to bottom point of shawl, (2 dc, ch 2, 2 dc) into bottom point of shawl; working along opposite side, rep from * to * to top edge, (2 dc, ch 2, 2 dc) into first st of top edge, (sc, ch 2, sc) in center dc of each sm-grp to center lg-grp, ch 2, (sc, ch 2, sc) in center dc of lg-grp, ch 2, (sc, ch 2, sc) in center dc of each sm-grp to last st, (2 dc, ch 2, 2 dc) in last st, sl st to first sc of edging.

Fasten off. Weave in ends. Block to finished measurements using method of choice (page 11).

> ≫ *Patients I've worked with have told me, "Each night, I pray for one more beautiful sunrise. Every morning, I smile." I find this extremely enlightening.*
>
> *--Rozetta Hahn*

Whimsical Boa

≫ *We all need a little whimsy in our lives. This soft wool-and-cashmere boa is just the thing to make your day brighter and put a smile on your face. Easy and quick to crochet, it naturally twists, accenting the crocheted fringe. It looks great worn long like a scarf or wrapped around your neck.*

By Janet Rehfeldt

SKILL LEVEL: Easy

FINISHED DIMENSIONS: 7½" x 48½" including fringe (after blocking)

FEATURED STITCHES

Back loop (bl)

Chain (ch)

Front loop (fl)

Slit stitch (sl st)

MATERIALS

2 skeins of Capra DK from Knit Picks (85% wool, 15% cashmere; 50 g; 123 yds) in color Flamingo

Size J-10 (6 mm) crochet hook or size needed for gauge

1 stitch marker

Tapestry needle

GAUGE

6 sts and 5 rows = 1" in patt

PATTERN NOTES

Sl sts can roll toward the back of your work. Tilt the work toward you so sts are easier to see and work into correct lp of sl st.

BOA

Row 1 (RS): Ch 9, bl sl st in 2nd ch from hook and in each ch, do not turn, ch 13, turn. Mark as RS of work—8 sl sts and 13 chs.

Row 2: Working in bottom hump of ch (page 7), sl st in 2nd ch from hook and in each of next 11 chs, fl sl st in each of next 8 sts, ch 13, turn—20 sl sts and 13 chs.

Row 3: Working in bottom hump of ch, sl st in 2nd ch from hook and in each of next 11 chs, bl sl st in each of next 8 sts, ch 13, turn—20 sl sts and 13 chs.

Rep rows 2 and 3 until approx 30" of yarn is left on second ball, ending with a row 2.

Next row: Working in bottom hump of ch, sl st in 2nd ch from hook and in each of next 11 chs, bl sl st in each of next 8 sts.

Fasten off. Weave in ends. There's no need for blocking; the boa will naturally roll in on itself.

Rose Star Scarf

> ❧ *The star stitch is one of my favorite stitches to crochet. It forms a beautiful pattern and creates a lush and cushy fabric using this wool-and-mohair yarn. The scarf can be worn long or wrapped around your neck several times, making it a great accent piece.*

By Janet Rehfeldt

SKILL LEVEL: Intermediate

FINISHED DIMENSIONS: 7¼" x 64½" (after blocking)

FEATURED STITCHES

Chain (ch)

Double crochet (dc)

MATERIALS

2 skeins of Birch from Hidden Valley Farm and Woolen Mill (75% coopworth wool, 25% mohair; 4 oz; 275 yds) in color Country Rose 🧶❷

Size L-11 (8 mm) crochet hook for beginning chain

Size I-9 (5.5 mm) crochet hook for scarf or size needed for gauge

Tapestry needle

GAUGE

8½ sts and 8 rows = 4" in patt with I hook

SCARF

Row 1 (RS): With L hook, *loosely* ch 142 sts. (Beg ch must be worked quite loosely since it tightens up with the st patt.) Change to I hook. Working in bottom hump of ch (page 7), YO, insert hook into 3rd ch from hook, pull through, YO, insert hook into next ch, pull through, YO, sk 1 ch, insert hook into next ch, pull through, YO, pull through all 7 lps on hook, ch 1 (this ch 1 forms an eyelet), *YO, insert hook into eyelet just made, pull through, YO, insert hook into same ch as last ch worked into foundation ch, pull through, YO, sk next ch, insert hook into next ch, pull through, YO, pull through all 7 lps on hook, ch 1; rep from * to end of row, turn.

Row 2: Ch 2, YO, insert hook into 2nd ch from hook, pull through, YO, insert hook into last eyelet of prev row, pull through, YO, insert hook into next eyelet, pull through, YO, pull through all 7 lps on hook, ch 1, *YO, insert hook into eyelet just made, pull through, YO, insert hook into eyelet of prev row used in last complete st just made, pull through, YO, insert hook into next eyelet of prev row, pull through, YO, pull through all 7 lps on hook, ch 1; rep from * to end, working final YO of last st into top ch of beg ch 2.

Rows 3–16: Rep row 2.

Fasten off. Weave in ends. Block to finished measurements using method of choice (page 11).

Pineapples in Silk Scarf

> ⫸ *The pineapple has been a symbol of hospitality, friendship, and warm welcome through the ages. I like to think it also means hope. This beautiful, decorative scarf with the pineapple motif is crocheted in luxurious 100% silk. It's the perfect gift for a loved one or caregiver, expressing your hope for hospitality, warmth, and friendship given and received.*

By Janet Rehfeldt

SKILL LEVEL: Intermediate

FINISHED DIMENSIONS:
5¼" x 68" (after blocking)

FEATURED STITCHES

Chain (ch)

Double crochet (dc)

Single crochet (sc)

MATERIALS

2 skeins of Mulberry from Louisa Harding (100% silk; 50 g; 136 yds) in color 04 Rose

Size G-6 (4 mm) crochet hook or size needed for gauge

Row counter (optional)

Tapestry needle

GAUGE

1¾ shells and 2¼ rows = 1"

SPECIAL STITCHES

Cluster (CL): YO, insert hook into next st, YO, pull lp through st, YO, pull through 2 lps on hook, YO, insert hook into same st, YO, pull lp through st, YO, pull through 2 lps on hook, YO, pull through rem 3 lps on hook.

Shell: (CL, ch 2, CL) in same st.

SCARF

Row 1: Ch 26, working in bottom hump of ch (page 7), CL in 5th ch from hook (counts as 1 dc, 1 ch, and 1 CL), sk 2 chs, shell in next ch, ch 3, sk 4 chs, sc in next ch, ch 5, sk 3 chs, sc in next ch, ch 3, sk 4 chs, shell in next ch, sk 2 chs, CL in next ch, (ch 1, dc) in last ch, turn.

Row 2 (RS): Ch 4 (counts as 1 dc, 1 ch, and 1 CL), CL in first ch-1 sp between dc and CL of prev row, shell in ch-2 sp of next shell, ch 3, sk next ch-3 sp, 6 dc in ch-5 sp, ch 3, sk next ch-3 sp, shell in ch-2 sp of next shell, CL in sp formed between beg ch 4 and first CL in row 1, ch 1, dc in 3rd ch of beg ch 4, turn.

Row 3: Ch 4, CL in first ch-1 sp, shell in ch-2 sp of next shell, sk next ch-3 sp, ch 1, (dc in next dc, ch 1) 6 times, sk next ch-3 sp, shell in ch-2 sp of next shell, CL in space between CL and beg ch 4 of prev row, ch 1, dc in 3rd ch of beg ch 4, turn.

Row 4: Ch 4, CL in first ch-1 sp, shell in ch-2 sp of next shell, ch 3, sk next ch-1 sp, (sc in next ch-1 sp, ch 4) 4 times, sc in next ch-1 sp, sk next ch-1 sp, ch 3, shell in ch-2 sp of next shell, CL in space between CL and beg ch 4 of prev row, ch 1, dc in 3rd ch of beg ch 4, turn.

Row 5: Ch 4, CL in first ch-1 sp, shell in ch-2 sp of next shell, sk next ch-3 sp, ch 4, (sc in next ch-4 sp, ch 4) 4 times, sk next ch-3 sp, shell in ch-2 sp of next shell, CL in space between CL and beg ch 4 of prev row, ch 1, dc in 3rd ch of beg ch 4, turn.

Row 6: Ch 4, CL in first ch-1 sp, shell in ch-2 sp of next shell, ch 5, sk next ch-4 sp, sc in next ch-4 sp, (ch 4, sc in next ch-4 sp) twice, ch 5, sk next ch-4 sp, shell in ch-2 sp of next shell, CL in space between CL and beg ch 4 of prev row, ch 1, dc in 3rd ch of beg ch 4, turn.

Row 7: Ch 4, CL in first ch-1 sp, shell in ch-2 sp of next shell, ch 6, sk next ch-5 sp, sc in next ch-4 sp, ch 4, sc in next ch-4 sp, ch 6, sk next ch-5 sp, shell in ch-2 sp of next shell, CL in space between CL and beg ch 4 of prev row, ch 1, dc in 3rd ch of beg ch 4, turn.

Row 8: Ch 4, CL in first ch-1 sp, shell in ch-2 sp of next shell, ch 7, sk next ch-6 sp, sc in next ch-4 sp, ch 7, sk next ch-6 sp, shell in ch-2 sp of next shell, CL in space between CL and beg ch-4 of prev row, ch 1, dc in 3rd ch of beg ch 4, turn.

Row 9: Ch 4, CL in first ch-1 sp, shell in ch-2 sp of next shell, ch 3, sc in ch-7 sp, ch 5, sc in next ch-7 sp, ch 3, shell in ch-2 sp of next shell, CL in space between CL and beg ch 4 of prev row, ch 1, dc in 3rd ch of beg ch 4, turn.

Row 10: Ch 4, CL in first ch-1 sp, shell in ch-2 sp of next shell, ch 3, sk next ch-3 sp, 6 dc in ch-5 sp, ch 3, sk next ch-3 sp, shell in ch-2 sp of next shell, CL in space between CL and beg ch 4 of prev row, ch 1, dc in 3rd ch of beg ch 4, turn.

Work rows 3–10 another 10 times.

Work rows 3–9 once.

Fasten off. Weave in ends. Block to finished measurements using method of choice (page 11).

Infinity Cowl

✎ *A lacy, twisted stitch creates an elegant yet cozy scarf that can be worn multiple ways: in a long single loop, wrapped over the shoulders, drawn up with a shawl pin as a stylish wrap, or wrapped double or triple around the neck as a large cowl. The two coordinating colors add extra interest. The wonderful feel of alpaca and silk, along with the varied ways of wearing this piece, will have you reaching for this accessory often.*

By Janet Rehfeldt

SKILL LEVEL: Intermediate

FINISHED DIMENSIONS: 16" wide x 76" circumference (after blocking)

FEATURED STITCHES

Chain (ch)

Double crochet (dc)

Half double crochet (hdc)

Slip stitch (sl st)

MATERIALS

A: 1 skein of Silky Alpaca Lace from Classic Elite Yarns (70% baby alpaca, 30% silk; 50 g; 460 yds) in color 2425 Rosa Rugosa ⓵

B: 1 skein of Silky Alpaca Lace from Classic Elite Yarns in color 2464 Cosmo

Size 7 (4.5 mm) crochet hook or size needed for gauge

1 stitch marker

Tapestry needle

GAUGE

8 cross sts and 8½ rnds = 4" in patt

COWL

With A, *loosely* ch 279. (Beg ch must be worked quite loosely since it tightens up with the st patt.)

Rnd 1 (RS): Working in bottom hump of ch (page 7), dc in 3rd ch from hook (counts as first 2 dc), hdc in sp between dc just made and ch 3 (cross st made), *dc in next ch, hdc in space between last 2 sts, working around post of dc just made; sk next ch; rep from * across to last ch, dc in last ch, hdc in space between last 2 sts. Being careful not to twist sts, bring ends together to form circle, sl st into 3rd ch of beg ch—138 twisted cross sts.

Rnd 2 (set-up rnd): Ch 1, dc in first st, PM for beg of rnd, hdc in space between dc just made and ch 1, sk next st, *dc in next st, hdc in space between last 2 sts, working around post of dc just made; sk next st; rep from * around to joining sl st from rnd 1, dc in sl st, hdc in space between last 2 sts worked. Do not sl st rnd closed. Cross sts should be offset from prev rnd, not sitting over each over.

Rnd 3: Sk first st, *dc in next st, hdc in sp between last 2 sts, working around post of dc just made; sk next st; rep from * around. Do not sl st rnd closed.

Rnds 4–16: Rep rnd 3. Change to B at end of rnd 16. Fasten off A, leaving 6" tail.

Rnds 17–32: With B, rep rnd 3. At end of rnd 32, sl st to first st of rnd. Do not fasten off.

EDGING

Rnd 1: Sc in same st as sl-st join on last rnd, (ch 3, sl st in first ch) (picot made), *sc in each of next 2 sts, make picot; rep from * around, sl st to first sc of rnd. Fasten off, leaving 6" tail.

Rnd 2: With A and working on opposite edge, attach yarn to base of dc, sc in same st as join, make picot, *sc in each of next 2 sts, make picot; rep from * around, sl st to first sc of rnd.

Fasten off, leaving 6" tail. Weave in ends. Block to finished measurements using method of choice (page 11).

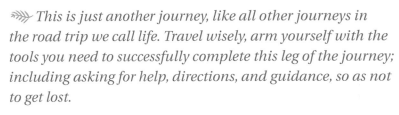

> ⫸ *This is just another journey, like all other journeys in the road trip we call life. Travel wisely, arm yourself with the tools you need to successfully complete this leg of the journey; including asking for help, directions, and guidance, so as not to get lost.*
>
> *~Anonymous*

Gossamer Lace Jacket

>>> *Soft mohair and silk create gossamer lace in this elegant yet simple jacket. It features a crossover front, forming an open V-neck, and a scooped neckline at the back. It's such a beautiful piece, you'll want to add it to your wardrobe for a must-wear cover-up on cool afternoons or evenings out. It's generously oversized for both comfort and easy on and off.*

By Janet Rehfeldt

SKILL LEVEL: Intermediate

FINISHED DIMENSIONS:
To fit bust: 36 (38, 40, 44)" when overlapped (after blocking)
Length: 21"

FEATURED STITCHES

Chain (ch)

Single crochet (sc)

Single crochet decrease (sc2tog); (page 10)

MATERIALS

5 (5, 6, 7) skeins of Kid Seta from Cascade Yarns (61% super kid mohair, 35% silk, 4% merino wool; .88 oz/25 g; 300 yds/275 m) in color 17 Primrose 🔲

Size I-9 (5.5 mm) crochet hook or size needed for gauge

Size H-8 (5 mm) crochet hook

Size 7 (1.65 mm) *steel* crochet hook

3 stitch markers

1 lightweight claw closure, approx 1¼" long

1 clear flat button, ⅝" diameter

Tapestry needle

GAUGE

9 clusters and 10 rows = 4" in patt with I hook

RIGHT FRONT

Row 1: With I hook, ch 89; working in bottom hump of ch (page 7), sc in 2nd ch from hook, *(sc2tog, ch 1) over next 2 chs, rep from * to last ch, sc in last ch, turn—43 clusters and 2 sc.

Row 2 (RS): Ch 1, sc in first sc, *(sc2tog, ch 1) over next ch-1 sp and sc; rep from * to last st, sc in last st, turn.

Rep row 2 until piece measures 8¾ (9, 10, 11)" from beg, ending on WS row.

RIGHT ARMHOLE OPENING

Next row (RS): Ch 1, sc in first st, work cluster over next 10 clusters, ch 34 (36, 36, 38) sts, sk 17 (18, 18, 19) clusters, PM to mark upper shoulder, work rem sts in established patt, turn.

Next row: Work in established patt to first ch; working in bottom hump of ch, *(sc2tog, ch 1) over next 2 chs; rep from * over ch sts, work rem sts in established patt, turn.

BACK

Work in established patt until piece measures 17 (18, 19, 21)" from right armhole opening, ending on WS row.

LEFT FRONT

Rep right armhole opening, PM to mark upper shoulder, then work in established patt until piece measures 8¾ (9, 10, 11)" from left armhole opening, ending with RS row. Fasten off.

FRONT EDGING

With H hook, attach yarn to RS at lower-right front edge, sc in same st as join, evenly space 86 sc sts along right-front edge to corner, work 3 sc in corner, evenly space 168 (174, 180, 186) sc sts along top edge of work, work 3 sc in corner, evenly space 86 sc sts along left-front edge, evenly space 168 (174, 180, 186) sc sts along bottom edge, 2 sc in same corner st as beg sc, fasten off.

SLEEVE

Make 2.

Row 1: With I hook and RS facing you, attach yarn to bottom of armhole opening, sc 76 (80, 80, 84) sts around armhole, turn—76 (80, 80, 84) sc.

Row 2: Ch 1, sc in first st, *sc2tog, ch 1; rep from * to last st, sc in last st, turn—37 (39, 39, 41) clusters and 2 sc.

Row 3: Ch 1, *(sc2tog, ch 1) over next ch-1 sp and sc; rep from * to last st, sc in last st, turn.

Rep last row until sleeve measures 21½ (22, 22¾, 23¼)" from beg, ending with WS row.

> ### Changing Sleeve Length
>
> Because the sleeves are worked from the armhole down to the wrist, you can easily stop them where you prefer. If you decide to make them longer, you may need additional yarn.

Next row (RS): With H hook, ch 1, sc in each sc and ch-1 sp across.

Fasten off. Sew underarm seams (page 10). Weave in ends. Block to finished measurements using method of choice (page 11).

FINISHING

Overlap lapels to form a V-neck and weskit-style front at bottom-front edge (see photo on page 30). Measure down from top neck at right-front edge approx 9" to 10" (or where you feel comfortable), sew hook side of closure to right edge. Sew opposite piece of closure about 7" to 8" from left edge at height where points at bottom edge are even and form a weskit-style front.

Measure down approx 10" from top edge along left-front edge. Using double strand of yarn and size 7 steel crochet hook, attach yarn with sl st, tightly work chain ½" long, attach with sl st 2 or 3 sts down (this forms button lp for clear flat button), fasten off, weave in ends.

Try on jacket and arrange lapels. PM on right front where flat button should go so jacket lays smooth and forms pointed weskit front. Sew flat button to WS of right front, aligning with button lp on left front.

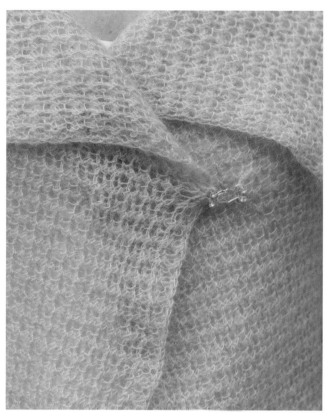

Gossamer Lace Bed Jacket

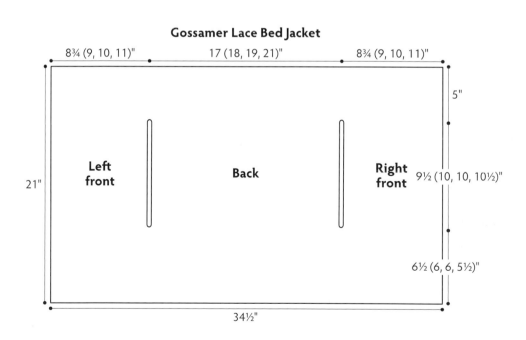

8¾ (9, 10, 11)"   17 (18, 19, 21)"   8¾ (9, 10, 11)"

5"

21"

Left front   **Back**   **Right front**   9½ (10, 10, 10½)"

6½ (6, 6, 5½)"

34½"

Textured Vest

This basic rectangular vest, crocheted from side to side, can be worn open and draped at the front or crossed at the lower-front edge and buttoned, creating a V-neck with a self collar for a finished look. The soft cotton, silk, and bamboo blend is light and comfortable, making this a very versatile piece.

By Janet Rehfeldt

SKILL LEVEL: Easy

FINISHED DIMENSIONS:
To fit bust: 32–34 (36–38, 42–44)" with overlap (after blocking)*
Length: 24"

Vest has a good amount of stretch; position buttons as needed for varying sizes.

FEATURED STITCHES

Chain (ch)

Half double crochet (hdc)

MATERIALS

6 (7, 8) skeins of CoBaSi from HiKoo (55% cotton, 16% bamboo, 8% silk, 21% elastic; 50 g; 220 yds) in color 021 Pink

Size 7 (4.5 mm) crochet hook or size needed for gauge

Size G-6 (4 mm) crochet hook

3 stitch markers

3 decorative buttons, 1" diameter

2 clear flat buttons, ½" diameter

Tapestry needle

GAUGE

20¾ sts and 14¾ rows = 4" in patt with size 7 hook

RIGHT FRONT

Row 1: With size 7 hook, ch 126, working in bottom hump of ch (page 7), hdc in 2nd ch from hook and in each ch across, turn—125 hdc.

Row 2 (RS): Ch 1, fl hdc in first st, *bl hdc in next st, fl hdc in next st; rep from * across, PM for RS of work, turn.

Rep last row until piece measures 11 (12, 13)" from beg, ending on WS row.

RIGHT ARMHOLE OPENING

Next row (RS): Work 22 sts in established patt, PM to mark shoulder, ch 50 (54, 58), sk 50 (54, 58) sts, work rem sts in patt, turn—125 sts.

Next row: Work in patt to first ch, work in patt across 50 (54, 58) chs, work rem sts in patt—125 hdc.

BACK

Work in established patt until piece measures 17 (20, 24)" from right armhole opening, ending on WS row.

LEFT FRONT

Rep right armhole opening, PM to mark shoulder, then work in established patt until piece measures 11 (12, 13)" from left armhole opening, ending with RS row.

Next row (WS): With G hook, hdc in each st. Do not fasten off.

EDGING

Left-front row 1 (RS): With G hook, sc in 36 sts along left-front edge, ch 2, sk 2 sts (buttonhole made), sc in each st to last 5 sts, ch 2, sk 2 sts, sc in rem 3 sts, turn.

Row 2: Ch 1, sc in each sc to ch-2 sp, 2 sc in ch-2 sp, sc in each st to next ch-2 sp, 2 sc in ch-2 sp, sc in rem sts, fasten off.

Right-front row 1: With G hook, attach yarn to lower-right front edge, sc in same st as join, sc in 22 sts, ch 3, sk 3 sts (buttonhole made), (sc 23, ch 3, sk 3 sts) twice, sc in rem sts, turn.

Row 2: Ch 1, *sc in each sc to ch-3 sp, 3 sc in ch-3 sp; rep from * twice, sc in rem sts.

Fasten off. Weave in ends. Block to finished measurements using method of choice (page 11).

Measure 4" along top neckline (long edge) on left front and sew one decorative button to WS of work. Fold lower-right front over left front, aligning bottom edges. Sew 2 large decorative buttons on RS of left front, about 6" or 6¼" in from edge, aligned with buttonholes. Sew clear flat button on WS of right front, aligned with buttonhole at bottom of left front. With vest buttoned, try on and arrange lapels and bottom edges. PM on right front where second clear flat button should go. Align front of vest to lay flat and sew button at marker on WS of right front. Overlap right front on left front, inserting buttons into buttonholes.

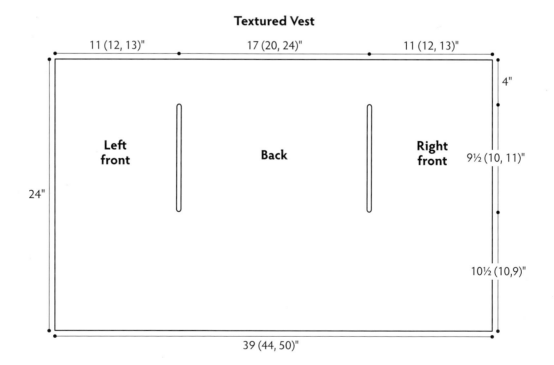

Textured Vest

Left front · Back · Right front

11 (12, 13)" · 17 (20, 24)" · 11 (12, 13)"

4"

9½ (10, 11)"

10½ (10,9)"

24"

39 (44, 50)"

Versatile Chemo Shrug

⋙ Soft, lacy, and very stretchy, this versatile piece is a shrug, shoulder wrap, and lap wrap in one. Buttons along the underarm turn it into a shrug that can be worn easily around IV and monitor tubing. The bands are worked into the pattern, creating self tapering at the cuffs for a nice fit. Wear unbuttoned, as a shoulder wrap or drape it over your lap. It works up quickly in a simple lace pattern using a large hook, and it's edged in crocheted seed stitch.

By Janet Rehfeldt

SKILL LEVEL: Intermediate

FINISHED DIMENSIONS:
18" x 43" (20" x 46" after blocking)

FEATURED STITCHES

Chain (ch)

Extended single crochet (esc); page 8

Single crochet (sc)

Slip stitch (sl st)

MATERIALS

2 (3) skeins of Shepherd Sock from Lorna's Laces (80% superwash merino wool, 20% nylon; 100 g; 430 yds) in color 507 Flamingo Stripe

Size K-10.5 (6.5 mm) crochet hook or size needed for gauge

2 stitch markers

8 flat buttons, 1" diameter

Tapestry needle

GAUGE

7 crossed sts and 13 rows = 4" in patt

Due to stretch in the stitch structure, smooth the piece on a flat surface when checking gauge and measure the piece often while crocheting. Stitches and rows should be slightly open and even.

PATTERN NOTE

Work sl sts loosely but not sloppily since you'll need to be able to work into them. The entire st patt is designed to be on the slightly loose side.

SHRUG

Foundation row: Loosely ch 155 (165); working in bottom hump of ch (page 7), sc in 2nd ch from hook, sl st in next ch, *(sc in next ch, sl st in next ch) (seed-st patt); rep from * across ch, turn—154 (164) sts.

Row 1: Ch 1, sc in first st, sl st in next st, (sc in next st, sl st in next st) twice, PM in last sl st made, esc in next st, *sk next st, esc in next st, esc in sk st; rep from * to last 7 sts, esc in next st, (sc in next st, sl st in next st) 3 times, PM in first sc of seed st, turn. Move markers with each row to mark first and last 6 sts of sleeve border—70 (75) crosses, 2 esc, and 12 seed sts.

Row 2: Ch 1, sc in first st, sl st in next st, (sc in next st, sl st in next st) twice, *sk next st, esc in next st, esc in sk st; rep from * to last 6 sts, (sc in next st, sl st in next st) 3 times, turn—71 (76) crosses and 12 seed sts.

Rep last 2 rows until piece measures 16 (18)" from beg, ending with RS row. Do not fasten off. Be sure to measure piece when it's relaxed, laid on a flat surface, smoothed out with sts slightly open.

TOP BAND

Rows 1–9: Ch 1, sc in first st, sl st in next st, *sc in next st, sl st in next st; rep from * across, turn—154 (164) sts.

Fasten off at end of row 9.

BUTTONHOLE BAND

Row 1: Working along beg foundation ch, attach yarn to WS of work, ch 1, sc in first st, sl st in next st, *sc in next st, sl st in next st; rep from * across, turn—154 (164) sts.

Rows 2–4: Ch 1, sc in first st, sl st in next st, *sc in next st, sl st in next st; rep from * across, turn.

Row 5 (buttonhole row): Ch 1, sc in first st, sl st in next st, sc in next st, *ch 2, sk next 2 sts, (sl st in next st, sc in next st) 3 times,* rep from * to * twice, ch 2, sk next 2 sts, sl st in next st, sc in next st, cont in established patt to last 29 sts; rep from * to * 3 times, then ch 2, sl st in next st, sc in next st, sk next 2 sts, sl st in last st, turn.

Rows 6–9: Work in established patt, working (1 sc, 1 sl st) in ch-2 sps on row 6. Fasten off at end of row 9.

Weave in ends. Block to finished measurements using method of choice (page 11).

Fold piece in half lengthwise. Place buttons on WS of work to align with buttonholes and sew in place.

> *The path we travel during our journey in life brings us face to face with many of life's challenges. You will find you have a strength within you didn't know existed and discover you can do beyond what is thinkable.*
>
> ~Judy Gutman

Wandering Rib Neck Cozy and Wrist Warmers

>>> *A soft silk-blend yarn is crocheted using a diagonal meundering rib. This oh-so-warm neck cozy buttons diagonally along the side edge, accenting the rib pattern. The matching wrist warmers will keep you comfy while leaving your hands free.*

By Janet Rehfeldt

SKILL LEVEL: Intermediate

FINISHED DIMENSIONS:
Neck cozy: 8" x 29" (after blocking)

Wrist warmers: 6 (7, 8, 9)" circumference* x 4" long

The warmers have approx 3" stretch to fit a variety of sizes.

FEATURED STITCHES

Back-post double crochet (BPdc); page 9

Chain (ch)

Front-post double crochet (FPdc); page 9

Single crochet (sc)

MATERIALS

Neck cozy

3 skeins* of Joey's Baby Silk from Queensland Collection (60% wool, 20% bamboo, 20% silk; 50 g; 164 yds/150 m) in color JBS-01 Baby Pink ②

3 buttons, 1¼" diameter

Wrist warmers

1 skein* of Joey's Baby Silk from Queensland Collection in color JBS-01 Baby Pink

4 buttons, 1" diameter

3 skeins of Baby Joey are sufficient to make both neck cozy and wrist warmers.

For both

Size G-6 (4 mm) crochet hook

Size I-9 (5.5 mm) crochet hook or size needed for gauge

Row counter (optional)

Tapestry needle

GAUGE

17 sts and 11 rows = 4" in patt with I hook

NECK COZY

Row 1: With G hook, ch 35, sc in 2nd ch from hook and in each ch across—34 sc.

Rows 2–4: Ch 1, sc in first st, sc in each st across, turn.

Row 5: With I hook, ch 2 (counts as first dc), FPdc in next st, *BPdc in each of next 5 sts, FPdc in each of next 3 sts; rep from * to last 8 sts, BPdc in each of next 5 sts, FPdc in each of next 2 sts, dc in last st, turn—34 dc.

Row 6 (RS): Ch 2, BPdc in each of next 3 sts, *FPdc in each of next 5 sts, BPdc in each of next 3 sts; rep from * to last 6 sts, FPdc in each of next 5 sts, dc in top ch of beg ch 2, turn.

Row 7: Ch 2, BPdc in each of next 4 sts, FPdc in each of next 3 sts, *BPdc in each of next 5 sts, FPdc in each of next 3 sts; rep from * to last 2 sts, BPdc in next st, dc in top ch of beg ch 2, turn.

Row 8: Ch 2, FPdc in each of next 2 sts, BPdc in each of next 3 sts, *FPdc in each of next 5 sts, BPdc in each of next 3 sts; rep from * to last 4 sts, FPdc in each of next 3 sts, dc in top ch of beg ch 2, turn.

Row 9: Ch 2, BPdc in each of next 2 sts, FPdc in each of next 3 sts, *BPdc in each of next 5 sts, FPdc in each of next 3 sts; rep from * to last 4 sts, BPdc in each of next 3 sts, dc in top ch of beg ch 2, turn.

Row 10: Ch 2, FPdc in each of next 4 sts, BPdc in each of next 3 sts, *FPdc in each of next 5 sts, BPdc in each of next 3 sts; rep from * to last 2 sts, FPdc in next st, dc in top ch of beg ch 2, turn.

Row 11: Ch 2, FPdc in each of next 3 sts, *BPdc in each of next 5 sts, FPdc in each of next 3 sts; rep from * to last 6 sts, BPdc in each of next 5 sts, dc in top ch of beg ch 2, turn.

Row 12: Ch 2, BPdc in next st, *FPdc in each of next 5 sts, BPdc in each of next 3 sts; rep from * to last 3 sts, BPdc in each of next 2 sts, dc in top ch of beg ch 2, turn.

Row 13: Ch 2, FPdc in next st, *BPdc in each of next 5 sts, FPdc in next 3 sts; rep from * to last 8 sts, BPdc in each of next 5 sts, FPdc in each of next 2 sts, dc in top ch of beg ch 2, turn.

Rep rows 6–13 until piece measures approx 27¾" long, ending with WS row.

Buttonhole Band

Row 1 (RS): With G hook, ch 1, sc in first st, sc in each st across, turn—34 sc.

Row 2: Ch 1, sc in first st, sc in each st across, turn.

Row 3: Ch 1, sc in first 3 sts, ch 3, sk 3 sts, sc in each of next 10 sts, ch 3, sk 3 sts, sc in each of next 9 sts, ch 3, sk 3 sts, sc in each of last 3 sts.

Row 4: Ch 1, sc in first st, *sc in each sc to ch-3 sp, 3 sc in ch-3 sp; rep from * to last 3 sts, sc in rem sts.

Row 5: Ch 1, sc in first st, sc in each st across, turn.

Finishing

Fasten off. Weave in ends. Block to finished measurements using method of choice (page 11). Referring to photo on page 40, wrap buttonhole edge around and pin to long edge at front. Space and sew 3 buttons in place.

WRIST WARMER

Left Wrist

Row 1: With G hook, ch 19, sc in 2nd ch from hook and in each ch across—18 sc.

Rows 2–4: Ch 1, sc in first st, sc in each st across, turn.

Change to I hook, beg with row 6 of rib patt in neck cozy, rep rows 6–13 until piece measures 5¼ (6¼, 7¼, 8¼)" from beg, ending with WS row.

Next row: With G hook, ch 1, sc in first st, sc in each st across, turn—18 sc.

Work last row 4 more times.

Fasten off. Fold piece in half with WS facing you. Place ending sc band over beg sc band, forming a circle with top of edge of sc band placed just below beg of rib patt. Use a running st to sew side edges only of sc bands tog. Evenly space and sew 2 buttons on band, sewing through both layers of the bands.

Right Wrist

Work as for left wrist, except work 5 rows sc for beg band, then beg with row 5 of rib patt in neck cozy. Rep rows 6–13 until piece measures 5¼ (6¼, 7¼, 8¼)", ending with RS row. Work 4 rows sc for ending band. Reverse sewing by placing beg sc band over ending sc band with top of edge of band just below beg of rib patt. Add buttons.

Weave in ends. Block to finished measurements using method of choice.

Suri Alpaca Beret and Fingerless Mitts

✦ Suri alpaca is known for its softness and warmth. This lovely beret uses a suri-and-merino blend for the band and brushed suri for the beret. The slouchy style is soft, warm, and comfortable. The fingerless mitts are the perfect chill chasers in soft-as-down suri with merino. The back-loop slip stitch gives the mitts lots of stretch to fit a wide range of hand sizes, and the simple construction with easy thumb opening make them a fast and easy project.

By Janet Rehfeldt

SKILL LEVEL: Easy

FINISHED DIMENSIONS:

Beret: To fit 20" to 23" head circumference (after blocking)

Fingerless mitts:

    Sizes: Small/Medium (Large/Extra Large)*

    Circumference: 6½ (8)"

    Length: 6½" (after blocking)

There is approx 2" to 2½" stretch to fit a variety of sizes.

FEATURED STITCHES

Back loop (bl)

Chain (ch)

Extended single crochet (esc); page 8

Extended single crochet decrease (esc2tog); page 10

Single crochet (sc)

Slip stitch (sl st)

MATERIALS

Beret

A: 1 skein* of Suri Merino from Blue Sky Alpacas (60% baby suri, 40% merino; 100 g; 164 yds/150 m) in color 412 Dawn (3)

1 skein of Suri Merino makes both bands for beret and the mitts.

B: 2 skeins of Brushed Suri from Blue Sky Alpacas (67% baby suri, 22% merino, 11% bamboo; 50 g; 142 yds/130 m) in color 907 Pink Lemonade (3)

Size G-6 (4 mm) crochet hook

Size H-8 (5 mm) crochet hook or size needed for gauge

1 stitch marker

Fingerless mitts

1 skein of Suri Merino from Blue Sky Alpacas in color 412 Dawn (3)

Size I-9 (5.5 mm) crochet hook or size needed for gauge

For both

Tapestry needle

GAUGE

Beret: 12½ sts and 11 rnds = 4" in esc with H hook

Mitts: 17 sts and 28 rows = 4" in bl sl st with I hook

BERET

Band is worked side to side in bl sts and top is worked in the rnd.

Band

Work bl sl sts slightly loose, but even. Sl sts tend to lie at back of the work. Tilt work toward you so sts are easier to see and work into correct lp of sl st.

Row 1: With A and G hook, ch 9. Bl sl st in 2nd ch from hook and in each ch across, turn—8 sl sts.

Row 2: Ch 1, bl sl st in first sl st, bl sl st in each sl st across, turn.

Rep row 2 until band measures approx 16½" in length.

Beret

Do not sl st rnds closed and do not ch 1 at beg of rnds unless instructed.

Rnd 1 (RS): Change to B, pivot band to work on long side edge of band. Evenly space 70 sc along band. Bring short ends tog to form ring, join with sl st in first sc. PM for beg of rnd. Sew band closed using invisible seam (page 10).

Rnds 2 and 3: Change to H hook, esc in first st, esc in each st around.

Rnd 4: *Esc in each of next 4 sts, 2 esc in next st; rep from * around—84 esc.

Rnd 5: *Esc in each of next 6 sts, 2 esc in next st; rep from * around—96 esc.

Rnds 6–9: Esc around.

Rnd 10: *Esc in each of next 10 sts, esc2tog; rep from * around—88 esc.

Rnd 11: Esc around.

Rnd 12: *Esc in each of next 9 sts, esc2tog; rep from * around—80 esc.

Rnd 13: Esc around.

Rnds 14–17: Rep rnds 12 and 13, working 1 less st between decs on dec rnds—64 esc at end of rnd 17.

Rnd 18: *Esc in each of next 6 sts, esc2tog; rep from * around—54 esc.

Rnds 19–23: Rep rnd 18, working 1 less st between decs on each rnd—16 esc at end of rnd 23.

Rnd 24: *Esc2tog; rep from * around—8 esc.

Fasten off, leaving a 6" to 8" tail. Thread tail through last rnd of sts and pull closed. Weave in ends. A soft brush will lift the hairs on your beret. Blocking is not necessary.

FINGERLESS MITT

Make 2.

Mitt

Mitt is worked side to side in bl sl sts. Work sl sts slightly loose, but even. Check your gauge often to make sure you're working evenly.

Row 1 (RS): With A and I hook, ch 27. Working in bottom hump of ch (page 7), sl st in 2nd ch from hook and in each ch across, turn—26 sl sts.

Row 2: Ch 1, bl sl st in first st, bl sl st in each st across, turn.

Rep row 2 until piece measures 3¼ (4)" from beg.

Thumb Opening

Row 1: Ch 1, bl sl st in first st, bl sl st in each of next 6 sts, ch 5, sk next 5 sts, sl st in next st, bl sl st in rem sts across, turn.

Row 2: Ch 1, bl sl st in first st, bl sl st in each st to ch 5, sl st in each ch, bl sl st in rem sts, turn.

Row 3: Ch 1, bl sl st in first st, bl sl st in each st across, turn.

Rep row 3 until piece measures 3¼ (4)" from thumb opening.

Fasten off. With RS edges facing each other, sew side seam using invisible seam (page 10). Weave in ends. Block to finished measurements using method of choice (page 11).

My Indoor Hat

≫ *When I was working on ideas for this book, a friend told me, "Design a hat for wearing indoors. Something a little loose . . . and make it pretty." This hat features delicate waves that flow seamlessly to the crown, and it's knit in soft, superfine yarn that feels wonderful. The cloche style is designed to be slightly loose fitting.*

By Janet Rehfeldt

SKILL LEVEL: Intermediate

FINISHED DIMENSIONS:

Sizes: Small (Medium)

Circumference: 20 (22)" unstretched (after blocking)

Hat has approx 2" stretch to comfortably fit variety of sizes.

FEATURED STITCHES

Back loop (bl)

Chain (ch)

Double crochet foundation (dcf); page 9

Extended single crochet (esc); page 8

Front loop (fl)

Single crochet (sc)

Single crochet decrease (sc2tog); page 10

Slip stitch (sl st)

MATERIALS

Model A (Small, shown on page 46)

1 skein of Comfort DK from Berroco (50% superfine nylon, 50% superfine acrylic; 50 g/ 1.75 oz; 178 yds/165 m) in color 2843 Kittens ⓘ3

Size F-5 (3.75 mm) crochet hook or size needed for gauge

Model B (Medium, shown above left)

1 skein of Comfort DK from Berroco in color 2723 Rosebud ⓘ3

Size G-6 (4 mm) crochet hook or size needed for gauge

For both

Size E-4 (3.5 mm) crochet hook for optional flower

8 stitch markers

Row counter (optional)

Tapestry needle

GAUGE

Small: 7 sts and 4 rnds = 1" in patt with F hook

Medium: 5 sts and 3¾ rnds = 1" in patt with G hook

SPECIAL STITCH

Puff stitch: YO, insert hook into both lps of next st, YO, pull through st, YO, pull through 2 lps, YO, insert hook into same st, YO, pull through st, YO, pull through 2 lps, YO, pull through 3 lps.

HAT

Do not ch 1 at beg of rnds. Do not sl st rnds closed unless instructed.

Rnd 1: With F for Small (G for Medium) hook, ch 3 (counts as first dc), work 104 dcf sts, sl st in top ch of beg ch 3 to close rnd—105 sts.

Rnd 2: *Esc in each of next 6 sts, sk 2 sts, esc in each of next 6 sts, (dc, puff st, dc) in next st; rep from * around—105 sts.

Rnd 3 (set-up rnd for patt): Bl esc 2 in first st, bl esc in each of next 4 sts, sk 2 sts, bl esc in each of next 6 sts, (dc, puff st, dc) in both lps of next st, *bl esc in each of next 6 sts, sk 2 sts, bl esc in each of next 6 sts, (dc, puff st, dc) in both lps of next st; rep from * around. leaving last dc unworked—106 sts.

> ### Pattern Hints
>
> The first esc st at beg of each rnd will always beg in a dc. The (dc, puff, dc) will always be worked in both lps of the prev puff st.

Rnd 4: PM in last dc of prev rnd, *esc in both lps of each of next 6 sts, sk 2 sts, esc in both lps of each of next 6 sts, (dc, puff st, dc) in next st; rep from * around, leaving marked dc of prev rnd unworked.

Rnd 5: PM in last dc of prev rnd, *bl esc in each of next 6 sts, sk 2 sts, bl esc in each of next 6 sts, (dc, puff st, dc) in both lps of next st; rep from * around, leaving marked dc of prev rnd unworked.

Rnds 6–11 (6–13): Rep rnds 4 and 5.

Rnd 12 for Small only: Rep rnd 4.

CROWN

Leaving beg-of-rnd marker in place, PM at bottom of each V on hat. Note that st will be either just before or just after actual V. Use same placement st for each marker. Move markers with each rnd. Move beg-of-rnd marker backwards as needed.

Rnd 1: Sc around—106 sc.

Rnd 2: *Sc in each st to 2 sts prior to next marker, sc2tog, sc in marked st, sc2tog; rep from * around—92 sc.

Rnds 3–12: Rep rnds 1 and 2—22 sc at end of rnd 12.

Rnd 13: Sc around. Remove all but beg rnd marker.

Rnd 14: *Sc2tog, sc in next st; rep from * around to last sc, sc in last sc—15 sc.

Rnd 15: Sc around.

Rnd 16: *Sc2tog; rep from * around to last sc, sc in last sc—8 sc.

Fasten off, leaving a 9" tail. Using tapestry needle, weave tail through last rnd of sts and pull tight to close top. Weave in ends. Block to finished measurements using method of choice (page 11).

> This is my crocheted version of an indoor hat designed with my friend in mind. You can find the knit version in the book *Knit Pink* (Martingale, 2013).

OPTIONAL FLOWER

Rnd 1: With E hook, ch 4, sl st in first ch to form ring, work 12 sc into ring, sl st to first sc—12 sc.

Rnd 2: (Sc, ch 4, sc) in fl of first sc, work (sc, ch 4, sc) in fl of rem 11 sc, sl st into bl of first sc from rnd 1—12 petals.

Rnd 3: Working into unworked bl of sc from rnd 1 and keeping petals to front of work and out of the way, (sc, ch 7, sc) in same sl st as join in rnd 2, work (sc, ch 7, sc) in bl of rem 11 unworked bl of sc sts from rnd 1, sl st in base of first sc of rnd.

Fasten off, weave in ends. Place flower where desired on hat and sew in place.

If desired, make 2 or 3 flowers for a nice cluster arrangement.

Fabulous Felted Hat with Brim

≫ *Extremely versatile and very stylish, this felted hat with a large brim will brighten anyone's day. Embellish with a ribbon, a purchased flower, or a hat pin to create your own unique sense of style.*

By Janet Rehfeldt

SKILL LEVEL: Easy

FINISHED DIMENSIONS:

Sizes: Small (Medium, Large)

To fit head circumference: 18–19 (20–22, 23–24)" after felting

Felting will custom fit hat to your head.

FEATURED STITCHES

Chain (ch)

Single crochet (sc)

Single crochet decrease (sc2tog); page 10

Slip stitch (sl st)

MATERIALS

Model A (shown on page 50)

2 (2, 3) skeins of Lamb's Pride Worsted from Brown Sheep Company, Inc. (85% wool, 15% mohair; 4 oz/113 g; 190 yds/ 173 m) in color M34 Victorian Pink

Model B (shown above left)

2 (2, 2) skeins of Cascade 220 from Cascade Yarns (100% Peruvian highland wool; 100 g/ 3.5 oz; 220 yds/ 201 m) in color 9478 Cotton Candy 4

For both

Size L-11 (8 mm) crochet hook or size needed for gauge

Row counter (optional)

Optional pin back for felted flower

Tapestry needle

GAUGE

10 sts and 11 rows = 4" in sc

> **Gauge Tip**
>
> Remember to keep a nice loose gauge. If you're slightly looser on gauge than stated in the instructions, it's fine; however, if you're tighter, you need to either go up in hook size or loosen your tension. The hat will not felt well if you crochet tightly.

CROWN

Do not ch 1 at beg of rnds. Do not sl st rnds closed unless otherwise instructed.

Rnd 1: Ch 1, work 4 sc into ch just below hook, sl st in first sc to close rnd, forming a circle. PM for beg of rnd—4 sc.

Rnds 2 and 3: Work 2 sc in each sc around—16 sc at end of rnd 3.

Rnds 4 and 5: *1 sc in next sc, 2 sc in next sc; rep from * around—36 sc at end of rnd 5.

Rnd 6: Sc around.

Rnd 7: *1 sc in each of next 2 sc, 2 sc in next sc; rep from * around—48 sc.

Rnd 8: *1 sc in each of next 3 sc, 2 sc in next sc; rep from * around—60 sc.

Rnd 9: Sc around.

Rnd 10 for Small: Sc around.

Rnd 10 for Medium and Large: *1 sc in each of next (9, 4) sc, 2 sc in next sc—(66, 72) sc.

Rnds 11–19 (11–22, 11–25): Sc around.

Next rnd: *1 sc in each of next 8 (9, 10) sc, sc2tog; rep from * around—54 (60, 66) sc.

Next rnd: Sc around.

BRIM

Rnd 1: *1 sc in each of next 2 sc, 2 sc in next sc; rep from * around—72 (80, 88) sc.

Rnd 2: Sc around.

Rnd 3: *1 sc in each of next 8 (9, 10) sc, 2 sc in next sc; rep from * around—80 (88, 96) sc.

Rnd 4: Sc around.

Rnd 5: *1 sc in each of next 9 (10, 11) sc, 2 sc in next sc; rep from * around—88 (96, 104) sc.

Rnd 6: Sc around.

Rnd 7: *1 sc in each of next 10 (11, 12) sc, 2 sc in next sc; rep from * around—96 (104, 112) sc.

Rnds 8–17: Sc around.

Rnd 18: Sl st in each st around.

Fasten off. Weave in ends, making sure your ending rnd has an even join so there's no lump in the brim after felting.

OPTIONAL FLOWER

Rnd 1: Ch 3, sl st in first ch to form ring, work 5 sc into ring, sl st in first sc—5 sc.

Rnd 2: 2 sc in each sc around—10 sc.

Rnd 3: (1 sc, 1 hdc, 2 dc, 1 tr, 2 dc, 1 hdc, 1 sc) in first st, sk next sc, *ch 1, (1 sc, 1 hdc, 2 dc, 1 tr, 2 dc, 1 hdc, 1 sc) in next sc, sk next sc; rep from * 3 times, PM in last sk sc—5 petals.

Rnd 4: Ch 2, holding petals to front to keep out of the way, work *(1 sc, 1 hdc, 2 dc, 1 tr, 2 dc, 1 hdc, 1 sc) in next unworked sc of rnd 2, ch 2; rep from * 4 times, working last petal into marked sc and omitting the ch 2. Sl st in base of first ch of beg ch 2 of rnd.

Fasten off and weave in ends. Flower can be felted or left unfelted.

FELTING

Set top-loading washer to hot, low water level and full agitation cycle. (You may need to add 1 or 2 cups of boiling water if your hot-water heater is set at a low temperature.) Place hat into zippered pillowcase to keep lint from clogging your washer. Add 1 tablespoon of mild detergent to water. Allow hat to agitate. Wearing *very heavy* rubber gloves to prevent burning your hands, check hat after about 5 minutes. Cont to agitate, checking every 3 to 5 minutes until hat appears to be size you want. Do not leave washer while felting. Once hat starts to felt it will felt very quickly. Reset agitation cycle if needed. When you're happy with hat size, set machine to rinse with cool or cold water and rinse item. Once washer sounds like all water has drained, stop the spin cycle. Do not allow hat to go through an entire spin cycle or it may leave permanent creases or folds. Check the fit again. If your hat needs more felting, reset washer and cont to agitate until felting is complete and hat fits.

BLOCKING AND SHAPING

Once you're happy with hat sizing, remove excess water by rolling hat in towels; squeeze or push out as much excess water as you can without twisting or wringing hat. Using a head form or rounded bowl that's just slightly larger than your head size, stretch hat down and over form or bowl, pulling on hat where brim just begins to form. Pull and shape crown and stretch out brim. When crown is shaped to your satisfaction, roll brim until you're happy with it. Leave hat to dry. This may take up to 2 or 3 days. Once dry, brush with a soft bristle brush to remove excess clumps of woolly fuzz.

For felted flower, sew a pin back on WS of flower and pin to hat.

Seed Stitch Headband and Mittens

⫸ *A superwash merino-and-cashmere blend make these mittens and headband both luxuriously soft and warm. The seed-like texture adds dimension and uniqueness to a great set you'll be bound to reach for often. The headband can be embellished with a crocheted or purchased flower pin.*

By Janet Rehfeldt

SKILL LEVEL:
Headband: Easy
Mittens: Intermediate

FINISHED DIMENSIONS:

Headband: 4" wide x 16 (18½)" circumference (after blocking)

Headband has approx 3" stretch to fit variety of sizes.

Mittens: 6½ (7½, 8¾)" circumference unstretched (after blocking)

Mittens have approx 2" stretch to fit variety of sizes.

FEATURED STITCHES

Back loop (bl)

Chain (ch)

Front loop (fl)

Single crochet (sc)

Single crochet decrease (sc2tog); (page 10)

MATERIALS

Headband

1 skein* of Superwash Merino Cashmere from Lion Brand Yarn (72% superwash wool, 15% nylon, 13% cashmere; 40 g/1.4 oz; 87 yds/80 m) in color 101 Blossom

Size H-8 (5 mm) crochet hook or size needed for gauge

1 flat button, 1" diameter

Mittens

2 (3, 3) skeins* of Superwash Merino Cashmere from Lion Brand in color 101 Blossom

Size F-5 (3.75 mm) crochet hook for mitten cuff

Size G-6 (4 mm) crochet hook mitten hand or size needed for gauge

3 stitch markers

For both

Tapestry needle

3 skeins make both mittens and headband in Small and Medium sizes for average-length hands (4 skeins for Large).

GAUGE

Headband: 3¾ sts and 3½ rows = 1" in patt with H-8 hook

Mittens: 4¼ sts and 4½ rnds = 1" in patt with G-6 hook

HEADBAND

Row 1: With H hook and leaving a 12" tail, ch 10, bl sc in 2nd ch from hook, *fl sc in next ch, bl sc in next ch; rep from * across, turn—9 sc.

Rows 2–7: Ch 1, bl sc in first st, *fl sc in next st, bl sc in next st; rep from * across, turn.

Row 8: Ch 1, bl sc in first st, (fl sc, bl sc) in next st, fl sc in next st, *bl sc in next st, fl sc in next st; rep from * to last 2 sts, (bl sc, fl sc) in next st, bl sc in last st, turn—11 sc.

Row 9: Ch 1, bl sc in first st, *fl sc in next st, bl sc in next st; rep from * across, turn.

Rows 10–13: Work rows 8 and 9 twice—15 sc at end of row 13.

Rep row 9 until piece measures 12½ (15)" from beg.

Next row: Ch 1, bl sc in next st, sc2tog, *fl sc in next st, bl sc in next st; rep from * to last 3 sts, sc2tog, bl sc in last st, turn—13 sc.

Next row: Ch 1, bl sc in first st, *fl sc in next st, bl sc in next st; rep from * across, turn.

Rep last 2 rows twice to 9 sts; then rep just the last row 6 times.

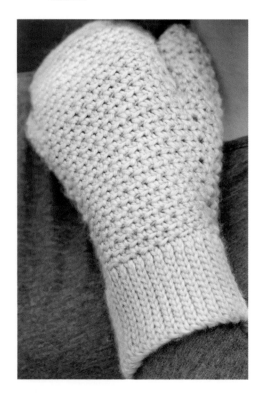

Flower Power

If you wish to embellish with flower, purchase premade flower pin or work the flower from "My Indoor Hat" (page 47) using size F or G hook. You could also make the flower from "Fabulous Felted Hat with Brim" with size F or G hook (page 49), but do not felt it.

Buttonhole row: Sc2tog, sc in next st, ch 2, sk next 3 sts, sc in next st, sc2tog—7 sc. Fasten off.

Using beg 12" tail on opposite end of headband and working into bottom of beg ch, sc2tog twice, sc in next 5 sts, sc2tog twice—7 sc. Fasten off.

Position button so headband fits comfortably, sew in place. Weave in ends. Block to finished measurements using method of choice (page 11).

MITTEN

Make 2.

Cuff

Row 1: With F hook, ch 13, bl sl st in 2nd ch from hook, bl sl st in each ch across, turn—12 sl sts.

Row 2: Ch 1, bl sl st in first st, bl sl st in each st across, turn.

Rep row 2 until cuff measures 6 (7, 8)". Do not fasten off.

Left Hand

Do not ch 1 at beg or sl st rnds closed unless otherwise instructed. You will end a rnd and beg next rnd with back to back fl or bl sc sts. This is normal to create alternating st structure.

Rnd 1: With G hook, evenly space 26 (30, 34) sc on long side edge, sl st in first sc to form ring and close rnd. Sew cuff seam (page 10).

Rnd 2: *Fl sc in next st, bl sc in next st; rep from * around. PM in first sc of rnd for beg of rnd, Move marker with each rnd.

Rnd 3: *Bl sc in next st, fl sc in next st; rep from * around.

Rnd 4: Rep rnd 2.

Gusset

Rnd 1: Beg with bl sc, work in established patt on 9 (11, 13) sts, (fl sc, bl sc) in next st, PM in fl sc of inc, fl sc in next st, (bl sc, fl sc) in next st, PM in last sc made, bl sc in next st, cont in established patt in rem sts of rnd—28 (32, 36) sc.

Rnd 2: *Fl sc in next st, bl sc in next st; rep from * around.

Rnd 3: Beg with bl sc, work in patt to first gusset marker, (fl sc, bl sc) in marked st, fl sc in next st, bl sc in next st, fl sc in next st, (bl sc, fl sc) in marked st, bl sc in next st, cont in established patt to end of rnd—30 (34, 38) sc.

Rnds 4–7 (4–9, 4–11): Work rnds 2 and 3 another 2 (3, 4) times, keeping in established patt on gusset sts—34 (40, 46) sc at end of rnd 7 (9, 11).

Rnd 8 (10, 12): *Fl sc in next st, bl sc in next st; rep from * around.

Next rnd: Beg with bl sc, work in patt to first gusset marker, ch 5, sk 11 (13, 15) sts, bl sc in next st, cont in established patt to end of rnd.

Next rnd: *Fl sc in next st, bl sc in next st; rep from * in each st and ch around. Keep first gusset marker for thumb opening, remove 2nd gusset marker—28 (32, 36) sc.

Work in established patt until hand reaches 1" less than middle or longest finger, ending with rnd 2 of patt.

Top Shaping

Fold mitten flat with thumb opening positioned correctly on hand. PM at each side edge. Move markers on each rnd to keep markers at side edges and decreases symmetrical. Cont in rnd 2 of established patt to center palm of hand, ending with bl sc, PM for new beg of rnd.

Rnd 1: Beg with bl sc, *work in patt to 2 sts prior to next marker, sc2tog, work marked st, sc2tog; rep from * once, cont in established patt on rem sts of rnd, working a bl in a fl and fl in a bl of prev rnd—24 (28, 32) sc.

Rnd 2: Beg with fl sc, *work in patt to 2 sts prior to next marker, sc2tog, work marked st, sc2tog; rep from * once, cont in established patt on rem sts of rnd—20 (24, 28) sc.

Rnds 3 and 4 (3 and 4, 3–5): Keeping in established patt, rep rnds 1 and 2 until 12 (16, 16) sts rem. Work to side edge; fasten off, leaving an 8" tail.

Right Hand

Work as for left hand to gusset. Fold piece so seam is on left, work in established patt to right-side edge, ending with fl sc. PM for new beg of rnd.

Rnd 1: Bl sc in first st, (fl sc, bl sc) in next st, PM in fl sc of inc, fl sc in next st, (bl sc, fl sc) in next st, PM in last sc made, bl sc in next st, cont in established patt in rem sts of rnd—28 (32, 36) sc.

Rnd 2: *Fl sc in next st, bl sc in next st; rep from * around.

Rnd 3: Bl sc, first st, (fl sc, bl sc) in marked st, fl sc in next st, bl sc in next st, fl sc in next st, (bl sc, fl sc) in marked st, bl sc in next st, cont in established patt to end of rnd—30 (34, 38) sc.

Rnds 4–7 (4–9, 4–11): Rep last 2 rnds 2 (3, 4) times, keeping in established patt on gusset sts—34 (40, 46) sc at end of rnd 7 (9, 11).

Rnd 8 (10, 12): *Fl sc in next st, bl sc in next st; rep from * around.

Next rnd: Bl sc in first st, ch 5, sk 11 (13, 15) sts, bl sc in next st, cont in established patt to end of rnd.

Next rnd: *Fl sc in next st, bl sc in next st; rep from * in each st and ch around. Keep first gusset marker for thumb opening,

remove 2nd gusset marker—28 (32, 36) sc.

Cont top shaping as for left hand.

Thumb

Rnd 1: With G hook, join yarn in first st of thumb opening, *bl sc in same st as join, fl sc in next st; rep from * on 11 (13, 15) sts, sc in base of each of 5 chs at top of thumb opening. PM in first sc of rnd for beg of rnd—16 (18, 20) sc.

Rnd 2: *Fl sc in next st, bl sc in next st; rep from * around.

Rnd 3: *Bl sc in next st, fl sc in next st; rep from * around.

Rep rnds 2 and 3 until thumb reaches middle of thumbnail, ending with rnd 3.

Next rnd: *Sc2tog; rep from * around, bl sc in last st 0 (1, 0) times—8 (9, 10) sc.

Next rnd: *Bl sc in next st, fl sc in next st; rep from * around.

Next rnd: *Sc2tog; rep from * around, sc in last st 0 (1, 0) times, do not fasten off—4 (5, 5) sc.

Cut yarn, leaving 6" to 8" tail, pull tail through last st. With tapestry needle, thread tail through sts at top of thumb, pull tight to close.

Sew top of hand closed (page 10). Weave in ends. Block to finished measurements using method of choice (page 11).

Cashmere Fingerless Gloves or Gauntlets

※ *Wrap your hands in pure cashmere and delectable textures with these cabled, gauntlet-style fingerless gloves. Whether you make them long or short, these gloves are definitely worth the effort. There's just nothing like pure cashmere to make you feel like the belle of the ball.*

By Janet Rehfeldt

SKILL LEVEL: Experienced

FINISHED DIMENSIONS:

Sizes: Small/Medium (Large/ Extra Large)

Circumference: 6½ (8)"

There is approx 3" stretch in circumference to fit a variety of sizes.

Length: 7¼ (10¼)"

FEATURED STITCHES

Back-post treble crochet (BPtr); page 10

Chain (ch)

Double crochet foundation (dcf); page 9

Double treble crochet (dtr)

Front-post treble crochet (FPtr); page 10

Half double crochet (hdc)

Slip stitch (sl st)

Treble crochet (tr)

MATERIALS

1 skein of Cashmere Lace Weight from Jojoland (100% cashmere; 2 oz; 400 yds) in color C222 Rose or color C234 Soft Pink

Size D-3 (3.25 mm) crochet hook or size needed for gauge

Size C-2 (2.75 mm) crochet hook for edging

3 stitch markers

Row counter (optional)

Tapestry needle

GAUGE

5½ sts and 3 rnds = 1" in cable patt with D

SPECIAL STITCHES

Cable 6 back (C6B): Sk next 3 sts, dtr in each of next 3 sts; working behind but not catching dtrs just worked, dtr in each of 3 skipped sts.

Cable 6 front (C6F): Sk next 3 sts, dtr in each of next 3 sts; working in front but not catching dtrs just worked, dtr in each of 3 skipped sts.

PATTERN NOTE

After working rnd 1 for first time, FPtr/BPtr sts are worked around FPtr/BPtr of prev rnd. On smaller size, PM in top of first FPtr/BPtr for beg of rnd. On larger size, PM in top ch of beg ch 2 for beg of rnd.

GAUNTLET

Make 2.

Cuff

Foundation rnd: Ch 3 (counts as first dc), work 34 (44) dcf sts, sl st in top ch of beg ch 3 to form a circle and close rnd—35 (45) dc.

Rnd 1: (Ch 2) 0 (1) times, FPtr around next st, C6B, *(FPtr around next st, dc in next st) 0 (1) times, FPtr around next st, C6B; rep from * 3 times, FPtr around last st 0 (1) times. Sl st in first tr for Small/Medium (in top ch of beg ch 2 for Large/Extra Large), PM for beg of rnd, turn.

Rnd 2: (Ch 2) 0 (1) times, BPtr around next st, C6F, *(BPtr

around next st, dc in next st) 0 (1) times, BPtr around next st, C6F; rep from * 3 times, BPtr around last st 0 (1) times. Sl st in first tr for Small/Medium (in top ch of beg ch 2 for Large/Extra Large), turn.

Rnds 3–10 (3–18): Work rnds 1 and 2 another 4 (8) times for short (long) length.

Thumb Opening

Next rnd: Work rnd 1 of established cable patt over 14 (19) sts (your next st should be FPtr, then a cable), FPtr around next st, tr in unworked lps behind post st you just worked, PM in tr, (inc made), C6B, tr in next st, FPtr around FPtr of prev rnd (this will be same st in which tr was just made), PM in tr, (inc made), cont in established cable patt on rem sts. Sl st in first tr for Small/Medium (in top ch of beg ch 2 for Large/Extra Large), turn—37 (47) sts.

Next rnd: Work rnd 2 of established cable patt over 14 (19) sts, ch 6 slightly loose but not sloppy, sk next 8 sts (1 tr, 1 cable, 1 tr all skipped), cont in established cable patt on rem sts. Sl st in first tr for Small/Medium (in top ch of beg ch 2 for Large/Extra Large), turn—35 (45) sts.

Remaining Hand Portion

Rep rnds 1 and 2 of established cable patt 3 times, working into ch sts on first rnd of rep.

Next 2 rnds: With C hook, hdc in each st around, do not turn work. Sl st in first hdc at end of last rnd. Fasten off.

Thumb

Rnd 1 (RS): With C hook for Small/Medium (D hook for Large/Extra Large), attach yarn in first tr at thumb opening, ch 2 (counts as first dc), C6F, dc in next tr, FPtr around post of st forming side edge of thumb opening (not st in rnd below); rotate piece to work into bottom of ch 6 of thumb opening, C6F, FPtr around post of st forming side edge of thumb opening (not st in rnd below); sl st in top ch of beg ch 2, do not turn, remove markers—16 sts.

Rnd 2: Ch 2, C6B, dc in next dc, FPtr around next st, C6B, FPtr around next st, sl st in top ch of beg ch 2, do not turn.

Next 2 rnds: With C hook (for both sizes), hdc in each st around. Sl st in first hdc at end of last rnd.

Fasten off. Weave in ends. Block to finished measurements using method of choice (page 11).

Picot-A-Boo Lace— or Not—Socks

🌿 *Pretty picot lace edging adorns these comfy socks, which are worked in soft washable wool. The sock features an easy afterthought heel and the single and double crochet stitches used for the leg and foot provide interest, making this a beautiful and quick project to make. Not feeling like lace? You can crochet these socks without working the lace edging for a simpler style.*

By Janet Rehfeldt

SKILL LEVEL:
Without lace edging: Easy
With lace edging: Intermediate

FINISHED DIMENSIONS:

Circumference of leg: 6½ (8, 9⅓, 10¾)" (unstretched, after blocking)

Circumference of foot: 6½ (8, 9⅓, 10¾)" (unstretched, after blocking)

Due to stitch structure, leg has approx 2" stretch.

FEATURED STITCHES

Chain (ch)

Double crochet (dc)

Double crochet foundation (dcf); page 9

Single crochet (sc)

Single crochet decrease (sc2tog); page 10

Slip stitch (sl st)

MATERIALS

With lace edging

2 (2, 2, 3) skeins of Wildfoote Luxury Sock from Brown Sheep Company, Inc. (75% washable wool, 25% nylon; 50 g/1.75oz; 215 yds/197 m) in color SY33 Crystal Pink

Without lace edging

2 (2, 2, 3) skeins of Wildfoote Luxury Sock from Brown Sheep Company, Inc. in color SY800 Sonatina

For both

Size E-4 (3.5 mm) crochet hook

Size D-3 (3.25 mm) crochet hook or size needed for gauge

3 stitch markers

Tapestry needle

GAUGE

5½ sts and 4½ rnds = 1" in patt with D hook

SPECIAL STITCH

Picot: Ch 3, sl st in first ch of ch 3.

SOCK

Make 2.

Work ch sts loosely but not sloppily when working cuff edging. Do not sl st rnds closed. Do not ch 1 at beg of rnds and rows unless instructed.

Cuff

Foundation rnd: With D hook, ch 3 (counts as dc), work 35 (43, 51, 59) dcf sts, sl st in top ch of beg ch 3 to form circle and close rnd. Do not fasten off. Sew cuff closed (page 10)—36 (44, 52, 60) dcf.

If not working lace edging, sk rnds 1–4 of lace edging and go to leg.

Lace Edging

Rnd 1: With E hook, ch 5 (counts as 1 dc and 2 chs), dc in same st as sl st join, sk next 3 sts, *(dc, ch 2, dc) in next st, sk next 3 sts; rep from * around, sl st in 3rd ch of beg ch 5.

Rnd 2: Sl st in ch-2 sp, (ch 3, dc) in ch-2 sp (counts as 2 dc), ch 2, *2 dc in next ch-2 sp, ch 2; rep from * around, sl st in top ch of beg ch 3.

Rnd 3: Sl st in next dc and ch-2 sp, (ch 5, dc) in same ch-2 sp (counts as dc, ch 2, dc), *(dc, ch 2, dc) in next ch-2 sp; rep from * around, sl st in top ch of beg ch 5.

Rnd 4: Ch 1, sc in first ch-2 sp, (ch 1 slightly loose, work picot, ch 1 slightly loose, sc) in first ch-2 sp, *(ch 1 slightly loose, work picot, ch 1 slightly loose, sc) in next ch-2 sp; rep from * around, sl st in first sc of rnd.

Fasten off, leaving 6" tail. Turn piece to work opposite edge of beg foundation round. With size D hook, attach yarn in top of first ch 3 of foundation rnd.

Leg

Rnd 1: *Sc in first st, dc in next st; rep from * around.

Rnd 2: Sc in first sc, PM for beg of rnd, dc in next dc, *sc in next sc, dc in next dc; rep from * around—36 (44, 52, 60) sts.

Rep last rnd until piece measures 4½" for sock with lace edging (5½" without lace edging) from top of dc foundation rnd.

Heel Opening

Rnd 1: Sc in first sc, keep marker for beg of rnd, loosely ch 18 (22, 26, 30), sk 18 (22, 26, 30) sts, dc in next dc, *sc in next sc, dc in next dc; rep from * on rem 16 (20, 24, 28) sts—18 (22, 26, 30) sts and 18 (22, 26, 30) chs.

Rnd 2: Sc in first sc, *dc in next ch, sc in next ch; rep from * across ch, dc in next dc on foot front, work in established patt across rem 16 (20, 24, 28) foot sts—36 (44, 52, 60) sts.

Foot

All rnds: *Sc in next sc, dc in next dc; rep from * around. Work in established patt until foot measures 2½" shorter than longest toe.

Toe Shaping

Work in patt to center back of foot, ending with a dc. PM in next sc for new beg of rnd. Fold sock flat so heel opening is placed correctly on back of sock foot (page 62). PM at each side edge of foot, moving markers with each rnd to keep at side edges. When working dec rnds, you may end up with a sc just before the dec and just after the dec. This is normal for keeping established patt.

Rnd 1: With D hook, work in patt to 2 sts prior to first side-edge marker, sc2tog, sc in marked st, sc2tog, work in patt to 2 sts prior to next side-edge marker, sc2tog, sc in marked st, sc2tog, work in patt on rem sts of rnd—32 (40, 48, 56) sts.

Rnd 2: Work in established patt (dc in dc; sc in sc) around.

Rnds 3 and 4: Rep rnds 1 and 2—28 (36, 44, 52) sts.

Rnd 5: *Work in patt to 2 sts prior to side-edge marker, sc2tog, sc in marked st, sc2tog; rep from * once, work in patt to end of rnd—24 (32, 40, 48) sts.

Rep rnd 5, having 4 less sts in each rnd until 16 (16, 20, 24) sts rem. Work to closest side edge, fasten off, and sew toe closed (page 10).

Heel

Fold sock flat so heel opening is placed correctly on back of sock foot. PM at each side edge of heel opening, moving markers with each rnd to keep at side edges.

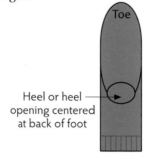

Toe

Heel or heel opening centered at back of foot

Sock folded flat

Rnd 1 (RS): With E hook, attach yarn at side edge of heel, evenly space 40 (48, 56, 64) sc sts, placing 20 (24, 28, 32) sts along each front half and back half of heel opening.

Rnd 2: *Sc to 2 sts prior to marker, sc2tog, sc in marked st, sc2tog; rep from * once—36 (44, 52, 60) sc.

Rep rnd 2, having 4 less sts in each rnd until 16 (16, 20, 20) sts rem. Work to closest side edge, fasten off, and sew heel closed (page 10).

Weave in ends. Block to finished measurements using method of choice (page 11).

Ballet-Style Slippers

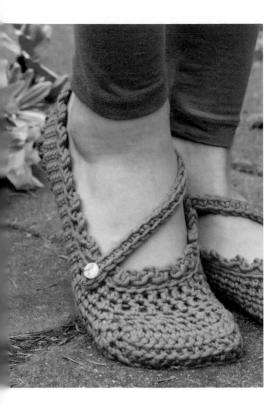

≫ Designed in the style of ballet flats, these comfortable slippers fit nicely on your foot and have the option of a diagonal strap. They're finished with a small scalloped edging for a little bit of extra flair.

By Janet Rehfeldt

SKILL LEVEL: Easy

FINISHED DIMENSIONS:

To fit woman's shoe size: 5–6 (7–8, 8, 9–10)* (after blocking)

See shoe size table at right.

> *≫ Live for the positive, the good, and the beautiful in life . . . it's out there, you only have to look.*
>
> *~Sonja R.*

FEATURED STITCHES

Back loop (bl)

Chain (ch)

Double crochet (dc)

Half double crochet (hdc)

Single crochet (sc)

Single crochet decrease (sc2tog); page 10

Slip stitch (sl st)

Slip stitch decrease (slst2tog); page 10

MATERIALS

1 skein of Worsted Merino Superwash from Plymouth Yarn Company Inc. (100% superwash fine merino; 100 g; 218 yds) in color 30 Bubblegum (4)

Size H-8 (5 mm) crochet hook or size needed for gauge

5 stitch markers

Tapestry needle

2 decorative buttons for straps, ½" diameter (optional)

GAUGE

5 sts and 6 rows = 1" in sl st patt

Shoe size	Foot length from heel to toe
5–6	8½"–9"
7–8	9½"–9¾"
9–10	10"–10¼"

SLIPPER

Make 2.

Sole

Row 1: Ch 14, sl st in bl of 2nd ch from hook and in each ch across, turn—13 sl sts.

Row 2 (RS): Ch 1, fl sl st in first st, fl sl st in each st across, turn.

Row 3: Ch 1, bl sl st in first st, bl sl st in each st across, turn.

Rep rows 2 and 3 until approx 1" less than length of foot or to length listed in table for shoe size, ending with WS row.

Next row (RS): Ch 1, slst2tog, fl sl st in cach of next 3 sts, slst2tog, fl sl st in each of next 4 sts, slst2tog, turn—10 sl sts.

Next row: Ch 1, bl sl st in first st, (slst2tog, bl sl st in next st) 3 times, turn—7 sl sts.

Next row: Ch 1, sc in each of next 4 sts, PM in last sc for center back of heel, sc in each of next 3 sts, evenly space 30 (32, 34) sc along side edge, sc in each of next 7 sts along toe, PM in last sc for center toe, sc in each of next 6 toe sts, evenly space 30 (32, 34) sc along side edge, PM for beg of rnd—80 (84, 88) sts.

Top of Foot

Count 20 (22, 22) sts backward, then forward from center-toe marker and PM on each side of foot. Move markers with each rnd. Do not ch 1 at beg of rnds. Do not sl st rnds closed unless otherwise instructed.

Rnd 1 (RS): Sc in next st, sc2tog, sc in marked st, sc2tog, sc to side edge marker, sc2tog 0 (1, 1) times, (sc in each of next 2 sts, sc2tog) 5 times, sc in marked toe st, sc2tog, (sc in each of next 2 sts, sc2tog) 4 (5, 5) times, sc in next st and marked st 1 (0, 0) time, sc in rem sts of rnd—68 (70, 74) sts.

Rnd 2: Sc to marker at center-back heel, sc2tog, sc to side edge marker, sc in marked st 0 (1, 1) times, (sc2tog, sc in next st) 5 times, sc in marked toe st, (sc in next st, sc2tog) 5 times, sc in marked st 0 (1, 1) times, sc in rem sts of rnd—57 (59, 63) sts.

Rnd 3: Sc to 6 sts prior to center toe marker, sc2tog, sc in each of next 2 sts, sc2tog, sc in marked st, sc2tog, sc in each of next 2 sts, sc2tog, sc in rem sts of rnd—53 (55, 59) sts.

Rnd 4: Sc to side-edge marker, hdc in next 5 (6, 6) sts, dc in next 7 sts, hdc in next 5 (6, 6) sts, sc in rem sts of rnd.

Rnd 5: Sc to side-edge marker, hdc in next 6 (7, 7) sts, dc in next 5 sts, hdc in next 6 (7, 7) sts, sc to center back of heel, sc2tog—52 (54, 58) sts.

Rnd 6: Bl sl st in each st around.

Rnd 7: *Ch 2, bl sl st in each of next 2 sts; rep from * around.

Fasten off, leaving 6" tail. Weave in ends. Block to finished measurements using method of choice (page 11).

Optional Diagonal Strap

Make length of ch sts to fit comfortably from just behind anklebone diagonally across top of foot toward front of foot, to about ½" below where little toe joins foot, plus 4 more chs. Sc in bottom hump of 2nd ch (page 7) from hook and in each ch across; fasten off, leaving 6" tail.

Sew 1 end on inside edge of slipper just behind anklebone at inside of your foot/leg. Place opposite end diagonally across top of foot toward front of foot, to about ½" below where little toe joins foot. Sew button or bead onto strap, sewing through strap and slipper. Weave in ends.

Rep for second slipper.

Trio of Facecloths

FEATURED STITCHES

Chain (ch)

Double crochet (dc)

Single crochet (sc)

Slip stitch (sl st)

MATERIALS

Shine Sport from Knit Picks (60% pima cotton, 40% model; 50 g; 110 yds) 3

Blushing Ingenue

A: 1 skein in color 6555 Blush

Pebbles

B: 1 skein in color 5083 Cosmopolitan

Shell-Lined Paths

C: 1 skein in color 6555 Blush

D: 1 skein in color 6563 Cream

2 closed-ring stitch markers or knitter's pins

For All

Size H-8 (5 mm) crochet hook or size needed for gauge

Tapestry needle

GAUGE

Blushing Ingenue: 14½ sts and 8 rows = 4" in patt

Pebbles: 14 sts and 8 rows = 4" in patt

Shell-Lined Paths: 15¼ sts and 10¾ rows = 4" in patt

⟫ *This trio of fabulous cotton face- or dishcloths is ideal for gift giving, fund raising, or using yourself. The cloths are quick to crochet and the soft cotton will baby your skin. Consider combining them with handmade soaps and lotions in a gift basket as a get-well gift or a thank-you for caregivers.*

By Janet Rehfeldt

SKILL LEVEL:
Blushing Ingenue and Pebbles: Easy
Shell-Lined Paths: Intermediate

FINISHED DIMENSIONS:
Approx 9" x 9" (after blocking)

Measuring a Square

Fold one bottom corner up toward the opposite top corner to form a triangle, aligning the side edges. When the edges meet correctly to form a triangle, you'll have a perfect square.

BLUSHING INGENUE

Row 1 (RS): With A, ch 32; working in bottom hump of ch (page 7), sc in 2nd ch from hook, *ch 1, sk next ch, sc in next ch; rep from * across ch, turn—31 sts.

Row 2: Ch 1, sc in first sc, *dc in ch-1 sp, sc in next sc; rep from * across, turn—31 sts.

Row 3: Ch 1, sc in first sc, *ch 1, sk next dc, sc in next sc; rep from * across, turn.

Rep rows 2 and 3 until piece measures 8½" from beg, ending with row 2. Do not fasten off.

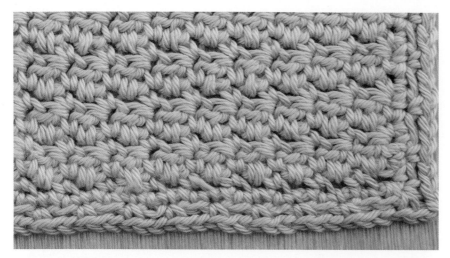

Blushing Ingenue

Pebbles

Shell-Lined Paths

Work edging as follows:

Rnd 1: (Sc, ch 1, sc) in first st (corner made), sc across 29 top sts to last st, (sc, ch 1, sc) in last st, evenly work 29 sc along side edge, (sc, ch 1, sc) in first st of beg edge, sc across 29 sts to last st, (sc, ch 1, sc) in last st, evenly work 29 sc along opposite side edge. Do not sl st rnd closed— 124 sc.

Rnd 2: (Sc, ch 2, sc) in first ch-1 sp, ch 2, *sk next sc, sc in next sc, ch 2*, rep from * to * to corner st, (sc, ch 2, sc) in ch-1 sp; [rep from * to * to next corner, (sc, ch 2, sc) in ch-1 sp] 2 times, sl st in first sc of rnd.

Fasten off. Weave in ends. Block to finished measurements using method of choice (page 11).

PEBBLES

Row 1: With B, ch 32; working in bottom hump of ch (page 7), sc in 2nd ch from hook, *dc in next ch, sc in next ch; rep from * across ch, turn—31 sts.

Row 2: Ch1, sc in first sc, *dc in next dc, sc in next sc; rep from * across, turn.

Rep last row until piece measures 8¾" from beg. Do not fasten off.

Work edging as follows:

Sc 2 in first sc, sc in 29 sts to last sc, 3 sc in last sc, evenly work 29 sc along side edge; working in bottom of beg ch, work 3 sc in first st, work 29 sc along bottom edge to last st, 3 sc in last st, evenly work 29 sc along opposite side edge, 1 sc in same st as beg 2 sc, sl st in first sc of rnd.

Fasten off. Weave in ends. Block to finished measurements using method of choice (page 11).

SHELL-LINED PATHS

Worked in 2 colors: 1 row in each color. Do not cut yarn after each row; instead, carry yarn up side edges. Keep closed-ring marker or knitter's pin in dropped lp of color you're not currently using to keep from unraveling as you work opposite color.

Row 1: With C, ch 32; working in bottom hump of ch (page 7), (1 sc, 2 dc) in 2nd ch from hook, sk next 2 chs, *(1 sc, 2 dc) in next ch, sk next 2 chs; rep from * to last ch, sc in last ch, drop lp from hook, placing marker or knitter's pin in lp. Do not turn—10 shells and 1 sc.

Row 2 (RS): Attach D in first sc of row 1, ch 1, (1 sc, 2 dc) in first sc, sk next 2 dc, *(1 sc, 2 dc) in next sc, sk next 2 dc; rep from * across to last sc, sc in last sc, drop lp from hook, placing marker or knitter's pin in lp, turn.

Row 3: Pick up C lp, ch 2, (1 sc, 2 dc) in first sc, sk next 2 dc, *(1 sc, 2 dc) in next sc, sk next 2 dc; rep from * across to last sc, sc in last sc, drop lp from hook, placing marker or knitter's pin in lp. Do not turn.

Row 4: Pick up D lp, ch 2, (1 sc, 2 dc) in first sc, sk next 2 dc, *(1 sc, 2 dc) in next sc, sk next 2 dc; rep from * across to last sc, sc in last sc, drop lp from hook, placing marker or knitter's pin in lp, turn.

Rep rows 3 and 4 until piece measures 8" from beg, ending with a C row. Do not turn.

Work edging as follows:

Rnd 1: With C, work 2 additional sc in last st of prev row (3-st corner made), evenly work 29 sc along side edge, work 3 sc in first st of beg ch, work 29 sc along bottom edge to last st, 3 sc in last st, evenly work 29 sc along opposite side edge, work 3 sc in first st of top edge, work 29 sc along top edge, change to D in last st, do not turn.

Rnd 2: With D, sc in each sc, working 3 sc in center sc of each corner; change to C in last st, do not turn.

Rnd 3: With C, sc in each sc, working 3 sc in center sc of each corner, sl st to first sc of rnd.

Fasten off. Weave in ends. Block to finished measurements using method of choice (page 11).

> ✹ *Never give up, never give in . . . not to the fatigue, not to the self pity, and most of all, not to this disease. Draw from the strengths of those who love and care for you when your spirits are at low ebb. Just don't give up. Ever.*
>
> *~Sue Peterson*

Facecloth and Hand Towel

FEATURED STITCHES

Chain (ch)

Double crochet (dc)

Single crochet (sc)

Slip stitch (sl st)

MATERIALS

1 skein* of Irish Linen from Interlacements (40% flax, 31% cotton, 29% rayon; 8 oz; 600 yds) in color Girly Girl

Size H-8 (5 mm) crochet hook or size needed for gauge

Size G-6 (4 mm) crochet hook

Tapestry needle

*1 skein will make 2 sets.

GAUGE

19½ sts and 18½ rows = 4" in patt with H hook

➤ Crocheted using a traditional woven (or linen) stitch in subtle changing hues from light pink to deep rose in a linen-cotton blend, this facecloth and hand-towel set are perfect for gift giving as well as personal use. The hand towel features a lovely fan edging for that little extra touch. The linen softens more and more with each washing.

By Janet Rehfeldt

SKILL LEVEL: Intermediate

FINISHED DIMENSIONS:
Facecloth: Approx 10" x 10" (after blocking)
Hand towel: Approx 10" x 21" (after blocking)

HAND TOWEL

Row 1: With G hook, ch 51; working into bottom hump of ch (page 7), dc in 3rd ch from hook and in each ch, turn—49 dc.

Row 2 (RS): Ch 2, 3 dc in first dc, sk next 3 sts, *(sc, ch 2, 3 dc) in next dc, sk next 3 sts; rep from * across, fasten off, leaving 6" tail.

Row 3 (RS): With H hook, attach yarn to bottom of first dc in beg ch; working in bottom of each dc, sc in first st, *ch 1, sk next st, sc in next st; rep from * across, turn—49 sts.

Row 4: Ch 1, sc in first sc, sc in ch-1 sp, *ch 1, sk next sc, sc in next ch-1 sp; rep from * to last st, sc in last st, turn.

Row 5: Ch 1, sc in first sc, ch 1, sk next sc, *sc in next ch-1 sp, ch 1, sk next sc; rep from * to last st, sc in last st, turn.

Rep rows 4 and 5 until piece measures 20" from beg, ending with WS row.

Next row: Ch 1, sl st in each sc and ch-1 sp across.

Fasten off. Weave in ends.

FACECLOTH

Row 1: With H hook, ch 40, sc in 2nd ch from hook and in each ch across, turn—39 sc.

Row 2: Ch 1, sc in first sc, *ch 1, sk next sc, sc in next sc; rep from * across, turn—39 sts.

Row 3 (RS): Ch 1, sc in first sc, sc in next ch-1 sp, *ch 1, sk next sc, sc in next ch-1 sp; rep from * to last st, sc in last sc, turn.

Row 4: Ch 1, sc in first sc, ch 1, sk next sc, *sc in next ch-1 sp, ch 1, sk next sc; rep from * to last st, sc in last sc, turn.

Rep rows 3 and 4 until piece measures 8½" from beg, ending with WS row. Do not fasten off.

Work edging as follows:

Rnd 1: With G hook, work 2 sc in first sc, sc in each sc and ch-1 sp to last sc, 3 sc in last sc, evenly space 36 sc along side edge, work 3 sc in first st of beg ch, sc in each st along bottom edge to last st, 3 sc in last st, evenly space 36 sc along opposite side edge, 1 sc in same st as first sc of rnd.

Rnd 2: Ch 2, 3 dc in next sc, sk 3 sts, *(1 sc, ch 2, 3 dc) in next sc, sk 3 sts; rep from * around, sl st to base of first ch in beg ch 2 of rnd.

Fasten off. Weave in ends. Block each piece to finished measurements using method of choice (page 11), creating points on edgings. Remember, linen will soften with each use.

Mark of Elegance Bookmark

➤ Elegantly mark your place in your favorite book with this quick-to-make bookmark. Dainty shells worked lengthwise, a combination picot edge, and your own special embellishments give this bookmark an intricate look.

Designed by Carol Lykins

SKILL LEVEL: Intermediate

FINISHED DIMENSIONS: 2½" x 8" (after blocking)

FEATURED STITCHES

Chain (ch)

Single crochet (sc)

Double crochet (dc)

Slip stitch (sl st)

MATERIALS

1 ball Classic 10 from Aunt Lydia's Crochet Thread (100% mercerized cotton; 350 yds) in color 0401 Orchid Pink 【1】

Size 1 (2.75 mm) *steel* crochet hook for edging

Size 2 (2.25 mm) *steel* crochet hook or size needed for gauge

1 stitch marker

Tapestry needle

Embellishments as desired (beads, ribbons, silk flowers)

GAUGE

1 shell and sc = 1" with size 2 steel hook

SPECIAL STITCHES

Shell: 5 dc in same st.

Clover picot: Ch 3, sl st in same sc, ch 5, sl st in same sc, ch 3, sl st in same sc.

Picot: Ch 3, sl st in same sc.

BOOKMARK

Row 1: With size 2 hook, ch 56, sc in 2nd ch from hook, sk next 2 chs, shell in next ch, sk next 2 chs, *sc in next ch, sk next 2 chs, shell in next ch, sk next 2 chs; rep from * to last ch, sc in last ch, turn—9 shells and 10 sc.

Row 2: Ch 3 (counts as first dc), 2 dc in first sc, sc in the center dc of next shell, *shell in next sc, sc in center dc of next shell; rep from * to last sc, 3 dc in last sc, turn.

Row 3: Ch 1, sc in first dc, shell in next sc, *sc in center dc of next shell, shell in next sc; rep from * to last 3 dc, sc in top ch of beg ch 3, turn—9 shells and 10 sc.

Rows 4–9: Work rows 2 and 3 another 3 times.

Next row: Ch 1, sc in first sc, *sk next dc, sc in each of next 3 dc, sk next dc, sc in next sc; rep from * across. Do not fasten off.

EDGING

Work edging in rnds. Do not join rnds with sl st.

Rnd 1: PM in last sc made for beg of rnd. With size 1 hook, 2 sc in same st as last sc of prev row (first corner made), (ch 3, sc in end of sc row) across top edge, 3 sc in first ch of left edge (corner made), ch 3, (sc in bottom lp of next shell, ch 3, sc in bottom lp of next sc, ch 3) across left edge, 3 sc in last ch of left edge (corner made), (ch 3, sc in end of each sc row) across bottom edge, 3 sc in first sc of right edge (corner made), (ch 3, sk 1 sc, sc in next sc) across right edge, ch 3, sc in first sc of rnd—44 ch 3 lps and 52 sc (including corner scs).

Rnd 2: Sl st in next sc, clover picot in same sc, sc in next sc, *2 sc in ch-3 lp, sl st in next sc, picot in same sc, 2 sc in next ch-3 lp, sl st in next sc, clover picot in same sc; rep from * around, always working a (sc, clover picot, sc) in each corner to last sc and ch-3 lp, sl st in ncxt sc, picot in same st, 2 sc in last ch-3 lp, sl st in first sl st of rnd—22 clover picot and 22 picot.

Fasten off. Weave in ends. Block to finished measurements using method of choice (page 11). Lightly starch to stiffen if desired. Add embellishments of your choice to make bookmark uniquely yours.

> ⫸ *I don't think of this as a battle you have to fight. It's just a path you have to take. You put one foot in front of the other until you don't have to walk the path anymore.*
>
> ~Lynda Lagodney

Cuddle-Me Pillow

⇒ A crunch stitch worked in the round gives this pillow an interesting twist that creates a richly textured diagonal pattern. The yarn is wonderfully soft, and the pillow is just the right size to cuddle with wherever you go. The zippered closure makes the pillow cover easy to take on and off for washing.

By Carol Lykins and Janet Rehfeldt

SKILL LEVEL: Easy

FINISHED DIMENSIONS:
12" x 16" (after light blocking)

FEATURED STITCHES

Chain (ch)

Half double crochet (hdc)

Half double crochet foundation (hdcf); page 9

Slip stitch (sl st)

MATERIALS

3 skeins of Nature's Choice Organic Cotton from Lion Brand Yarn (100% organic cotton; 3 oz/85 g; 103 yd/94 m) in color 101 Strawberry

Size K-10½ (6.5 mm) crochet hook or size needed for gauge

1 stitch marker

Tapestry needle

9" zipper in matching color,

Sewing needle and thread in matching color

Pillow form, 12" x 16"

GAUGE

10 sts and 12½ rnds = 4" in patt

PILLOW COVER

Pillow cover is worked in the rnd with foundation rnd forming a pocket. Do not sl st rnds closed or ch 1 at beg of rnds unless instructed.

Foundation rnd: Ch 2 (counts as hdc), work 29 hdcf sts. Working in both bottom lps of 30 hdcf sts just made, hdc in each st across to beg ch 2, hdc in the first ch of beg ch 2—60 hdc.

Rnd 1: Sl st in top ch of beg ch 2 of foundation rnd, PM for beg of rnd, hdc in next hdc, *sl st in next hdc, hdc in next hdc; rep from * around.

Rnd 2: Hdc in first st, sl st in next st, *hdc in next st, sl st in next st; rep from * around.

Rnd 3: Sl st in first st, hdc in next st, *sl st in next st, hdc in next st; rep from * around.

Rep rnds 2 and 3 until pillow measures 15¾" high, ending at a side edge.

Fasten off, weave in ends. Block to finished measurements using method of choice (page 11). Be careful; stitch structure and cotton stretches easily.

SEWING IN ZIPPER

Center zipper along open end of pillow. With zipper open, pin one edge of pillow to one side of zipper. Then pin other side of zipper to other side of pillow. Place pins horizontally, not vertically, so zipper doesn't ripple. With sewing needle and thread, sew zipper in place using small sewing stitches and keeping fabric slightly away from zipper teeth. Sew rem section of pillow at each end of zipper closed. Insert pillow form and cuddle.

Coffee Cup and Travel Mug Cozies

✺ *Keep your favorite beverage hot and cozy whether at home or on the go with these stylish fitted coffee cup and travel mug warmers. The size can be customized for your travel or to-go mug by eliminating the decreases for a straight style.*

By Carol Lykins and Janet Rehfeldt

SKILL LEVEL: Intermediate

FINISHED DIMENSIONS:

Coffee cup cozy: Fits 8 to 10 oz coffee cup (with handle)

Travel mug cozy: Fits 16 to 20 oz, tapered travel mug

FEATURED STITCHES

Chain (ch)

Double crochet (dc)

Double crochet foundation (dcf); page 9

Front-post double crochet (FPdc); page 9

Front loop (fl)

Half double crochet (hdc)

Half double crochet decrease (hdc2tog); page 10

Half double crochet foundation (hdcf); page 9

Slip stitch (sl st)

MATERIALS

1 ball* of Fashion by Aunt Lydia's Crochet Thread (100% mercerized cotton; 150 yd/137 m) in color 775 Warm Rose

Size E-4 (3.5 mm) crochet hook or size needed for gauge

Size D-3 (3.25 mm) crochet hook

1 toggle button for Coffee Cup Cozy, 1½" long

1 stitch marker

Tapestry needle

1 ball will make both cozies.

GAUGE

6 hdc = 1" with E hook

TRAVEL MUG COZY

Work FPdc in rnd below unless otherwise instructed. Do not join rnds unless otherwise instructed. Move markers up with each rnd.

Upper Cuff

Foundation rnd: With E hook, ch 3 (counts as first dc), work 45 dcf sts, sl st in top ch of beg ch 3 to close rnd and form ring—46 dc.

Rnd 1: FPdc around first st, PM for beg of rnd, hdc in next st, *FPdc around next st, hdc in next st; rep from * around.

Rnds 2 and 3: *FPdc around next FPdc, hdc in next st; rep from * around, sl st in first FPdc of rnd at end of rnd 3.

Sleeve

Rnd 1: Hdc2tog over first 2 sts, hdc in each of next 21 sts, hdc2tog over next 2 sts, hdc in rem sts—44 st.

Rnd 2: Hdc in each st around.

Rnd 3: *FPdc around each of next 2 sts in rnd 1, hdc in each of next 2 sts; rep from * around—22 FPdc and 22 hdc.

Rnd 4: Hdc in each st around, sl st in first st to close rnd.

Rnd 5: *FPdc around each of next 2 FPdc in rnd 3, hdc in each of next 2 sts; rep from * around.

Rnd 6: *Hdc in each of next 6 sts, hdc2tog, hdc in each of next 10 sts, hdc2tog; rep from * to last 4 sts, hdc in each of last 4 sts, sl st in first st to close rnd—40 hdc.

Rnd 7: FPdc around each of next 2 FPdc, hdc in each of next 2 sts, FPdc around each of next 2 FPdc, hdc in the next st, *(FPdc around each of next 2 FPdc, hdc in each of next 2 sts) twice, FPdc around each of the next 2 FPdc, hdc in next st; FPdc around each of the next 2 FPdc, hdc in each of next 2 sts*, FPdc around each of the next 2 FPdc, hdc in next st; rep from * to * once—22 FPdc and 18 hdc.

Rnd 8: Hdc in each st around, sl st in first hdc of rnd to close rnd—40 hdc.

Rnd 9: Rep rnd 7.

Rnd 10: Hdc in each of next 6 sts, hdc2tog, (hdc in each of next 5 sts, hdc2tog) twice, hdc in each of next 9 sts, hdc2tog, hdc in the last 7 sts, sl st in first st to close rnd—36 sts.

Rnd 11: FPdc around each of next 2 FPdc, hdc in each of next 2 sts, *FPdc around each of next 2 FPdc, hdc in next st*, rep from * to * 5 times, FPdc around each of next 2 FPdc, hdc in each of next 2 sts; rep from * to * twice, then FPdc around each of next 2 FPdc, hdc in each of next 2 sts—22 FPdc and 14 hdc.

Rnd 12: Hdc in each st around, sl st in first hdc to close rnd.

Rnd 13: Rep rnd 11.

Lower Cuff

Rnd 1: *Hdc2tog over next 2 sts, hdc in each of next 7 sts; rep from * 3 times—32 hdc.

Rnd 2: Hdc in each st around, sl st to close rnd.

Rnd 3: *FPdc around next st of rnd 1, hdc in next st; rep from * around.

Rnd 4: *FPdc around next FPdc, hdc in next st; rep from * around, sl st in first dc of rnd.

Fasten off. Weave in ends. Sew open edge at top of cuff closed (page 10).

COFFEE CUP COZY

Cozy is worked back and forth and edging is worked in the rnd.

Cozy

Foundation row: With E hook, ch 2 (counts as first hdc), work 45 hdcf sts, turn—46 hdc.

Row 1: Ch 2 (counts as first hdc), hdc in each st across, work last hdc in top ch of beg ch 2, turn.

Row 2: Ch 2, hdc in next st, *FPdc around each of next 2 sts in row 1, hdc in each of next 2 sts; rep from * across, working last hdc in top ch of beg ch 2, turn—22 FPdc and 24 hdc.

Row 3: Ch 2, hdc in next st; hdc in each st across, working last hdc in top ch of beg ch 2, turn.

Row 4: Ch 2, hdc in next st, *FPdc around each of next 2 FPdc, hdc in next 2 sts; rep from * across, working last hdc in top ch of beg ch 2, turn.

Work rows 3 and 4 another 4 times. Do not turn.

Edging and Button Loop

Edging is worked in the round.

Rnd 1: With D hook and RS of work facing you, work 12 sc evenly spaced in end rows of cozy, PM in first sc for beg of rnd, work 3 sc at corner, sc in each st across top edge to next corner, work 3 sc at corner, work 12 sc evenly spaced in end rows to next corner, work 3 sc at corner, sc in each st across bottom edge to beg sc, 2 sc in same st as beg sc, sl st in beg sc.

Rnd 2 (RS, joining rnd): Ch 3, fold cozy with RS facing you into a circle with short ends aligned from top to bottom, sl st from back in middle sc of corresponding corner (this is now bottom of cozy), turn work to sc back across each ch of the ch 3, sc in each of next 14 sts on left edge, ch 3, sl st in corresponding corner of right side of cozy (this is top of cozy), sc in each of next 5 sts, ch 9, sk next 3 sts, sc in next st, sc in each of next 5 sts, sl in next st, turn.

Rnd 3 (WS): Sl st in fl only in each of next 6 sts, sc in each of next 9 chs, sl st in fl only in each of next 5 sts, sl st in each ch of ch 3. Fasten off.

Weave in ends. Attach button on left side of cozy. Slip cup handle between opening, and then slip cozy around cup and button.

Divine Comfort Throw

This is a wonderfully comfortable and snuggly throw. Worked in a simple V stitch with a large hook, this project is quick to make and positively gorgeous. You'll definitely want to cuddle up with a good book or some favorite music in divine comfort.

By Janet Rehfeldt

SKILL LEVEL: Easy

FINISHED DIMENSIONS:
36" x 48" (after light blocking)

FEATURED STITCHES

Chain (ch)

Extended single crochet (esc); page 8

Single crochet (sc)

Slip stitch (sl st)

MATERIALS

6 skeins of Divine from Patons (76.5% acrylic, 10.5% wool, 10.5% mohair, 2.5% polyester; 3.5 oz/100 g; 142 yds/129 m) in color 06406 Chantilly Rose

Size L-11 (8 mm) crochet hook

Size N/P-15 (10 mm) crochet hook or size needed for gauge

1 stitch marker

Tapestry needle

GAUGE

3 V sts and 5 rows = 4" in patt with N hook

THROW

Work beg ch quite loosely to accommodate the st patt and loft of yarn. Measure on a flat surface since yarn and st tend to stretch.

Row 1 (RS): With N hook, ch 53 *very loosely*. Working in bottom hump of ch (page 7), esc in 2nd ch from hook, sk next ch, *(esc, ch 1, esc) in next ch, sk next ch;

rep from * across to last ch, esc in last ch, turn—25 V sts and 2 esc.

Row 2: Ch 1, esc in first st, *(esc, ch 1, esc) in next esc, sk next ch-1 and esc; rep from * across to last st, esc in last esc, turn.

Rep row 2 until piece measures approx 44½" from beg, ending with WS row. Do not fasten off.

EDGING

Work sc slightly loose but not sloppy. Move beg-of-rnd marker on each rnd.

Rnd 1 (RS): With L hook, work 3 sc in first esc; skipping ch-1 sps, sc 50 in each esc across top edge to last st, work 3 sc in last st (corner made), evenly space 80 sc sts along side edge; working into bottom of beg ch, work 3 sc in first st, sc 50 along bottom edge to last st, work 3 sc in last st, evenly space sc 80 along rem side edge, do not sl st closed—272 sc.

Rnds 2–4: Sc 3 in first sc of rnd, PM in first sc for beg of rnd, sc in each sc; working 3 sc in center sc of each corner, sl st in first sc of rnd.

Fasten off. Weave ends. Block lightly to finished measurements using method of choice (page 11).

Variation-on-a-Theme Throw

Shades of pinks, ranging from light rose to bright fuchsia and ending with deep rose, are crocheted in bands. This throw uses a variation on a shell stitch for each band to create a unique throw, which will wrap you up in soft warmth and comfort.

By Janet Rehfeldt

SKILL LEVEL: Intermediate

FINISHED DIMENSIONS: 36" x 46" (after blocking)

Whisper to me of shell-lined paths, of cresting waves, and gulls soaring past. Whisper to me of the deep deep sea . . . the sea, the beautiful healing sea.

~Janet R.

FEATURED STITCHES

Chain (ch)

Double crochet (dc)

Front-post double crochet (FPdc); page 9

Half double crochet (hdc)

Single crochet (sc)

MATERIALS

Tonic from Jojoland (85% acrylic, 15% wool; 3.5oz/100 g; 220 yds/200 m;) **4**

A: 2 skeins in color AW116

B: 2 skeins in color AW124

C: 2 skeins in color AW136

D: 2 skeins in color AW144

E: 2 skeins in color AW308

Size J-10 (6 mm) crochet hook or size needed for gauge

Size I-9 (5.5 mm) crochet hook

1 stitch marker

Tapestry needle

GAUGE

5¾ shells = 4" in patt A with J hook

5¾ shells = 4" in patt B with J hook

2¾ full shell = 4" in patt C with J hook

7 mini shells = 4" in patt D with J hook

THROW

The throw is worked in four stitch patts separated by a divider patt, and then edged in same patt as divider.

First Band

Foundation row: With A, ch 190; working in bottom hump of ch (page 7), sc in 2nd ch from hook and in each ch, turn—189 sc.

Row 1 (RS): Ch 1, hdc in first sc, sk next sc, (sc, ch 2, sc) in next sc, *sk next 2 sc, (sc, ch 2, sc) in next sc; rep from * across to last 3 sts, sk next 2 sts, hdc in last sc, turn.

From left to right: first, second, third, and fourth bands.

Row 2: Ch 3 (counts as first dc), *3 hdc in ch-2 sp (shell made); rep from * across to last st, dc in hdc, turn.

Row 3: Ch 1, hdc in first dc, (sc, ch 2, sc) in center hdc of each shell across to last st, hdc in top ch of beg ch 3, PM about midsection for RS of work, turn.

Rep rows 2 and 3 until first band measures 7" from beg, ending with WS row and changing to E in last st. Cut A, leaving 6" tail for weaving in.

Divider Pattern

Row 1 (RS): With E and I hook, sc in first st, sc in each hdc across, sc in top ch of beg ch 2 of prev row, turn.

Row 2: Ch 1, sc in first st, *ch 1, sk next st, sc in next st; rep from * across, turn.

Rows 3–6: Rep row 2, changing to B in last st of row 6. Cut E, leaving a 6" tail for weaving in.

Second Band

Row 1 (RS): With B and J hook, sc in first st, *sc in top 2 lps of

next ch st, sc in next sc; rep from * across, turn.

Row 2: Ch 1, (1 sc, 2 dc) in first sc, sk next 2 sc, *(1 sc, 2 dc) in next sc, sk next 2 sc; rep from * to last st, sc in last sc, turn.

Row 3: Ch 1, (1 sc, 2 dc) in first sc, sk next 2 dc, *(1 sc, 2 dc) in next sc, sk next 2 dc; rep from * across to end, sc in last sc, turn.

Rep row 3 until second band measures 8", ending with WS row and changing to E in last st. Cut B, leaving 6" tail for weaving in.

With E and I hook, sc in each sc and dc across, then work rows 2–6 of divider patt, changing to C in last sc of row 6. Cut E, leaving 6" tail for weaving in.

Third Band

Row 1 (RS): With C and J hook, sc in first sc, *sc in top 2 lps of next ch, sc in next sc; rep from * across, turn.

Row 2: Ch 1, sc in first sc, *sk next 2 sc, 5 dc in next sc, sk 2 sc, sc in next sc; rep from * across, turn.

Row 3: Ch 2 (counts as first dc), 2 dc in first st, *sk next 2 dc, sc in next dc, sk next 2 dc, 5 dc in next sc; rep from * across, ending with only 3 dc in last sc, turn.

Row 4: Ch 1, sc in first dc, *sk next 2 dc, 5 dc in next sc, sk next 2 dc, sc in next dc; rep from * across end with sc in top ch of beg ch 2 of prev row, turn.

Rep rows 3 and 4 until third band measures 7", ending with WS row, turn.

Next row: Ch 3 (counts as first dc), *hdc in next dc, sc in next dc, sl st in next dc, sc in next dc, hdc in next dc, dc in next sc; rep from * across. Cut C, leaving 6" tail for weaving in.

With E and size I hook, join in first st on RS of work, sc in each st across, then work rows 2–6 of divider patt, change to D in last st of row 6. Cut E, leaving 6" tail for weaving in.

Fourth Band

Row 1 (RS): With D and J hook, sc in first sc, *sc in top 2 lps of next ch st, sc in next sc; rep from * across, turn.

Row 2: Ch 1, (sc, ch 1, sc) in first sc, sk next 2 sc, *(sc, ch 1, sc) in next sc, sk next 2 sc; rep from * across to last st, sc in last st, turn.

Row 3: Ch 1, (hdc, ch 1, hdc) in first sc, sk next sc and ch-1 sp, *(hdc, ch 1, hdc) in next sc, sk next sc and ch-1 sp; rep from * to last st, hdc in last sc, turn.

Row 4: Ch 1, (sc, ch 1, sc) in first hdc, sk next hdc and ch-1 sp, *(sc, ch 1, sc) in next hdc, sk next hdc and ch-1 sp; rep from * across to last st, sc in last st, turn.

Rep rows 3 and 4 until fourth band measures 7", ending with WS row and changing to E in last st. Cut D, leaving 6" tail for weaving in.

Edging

Although worked around edge, turn after each rnd.

Rnd 1 (RS): Change to E and cont working with J hook, work 3 sc in first sc (corner made); skipping each ch-1 sp, sc in each sc across edge to last st, work 3 sc in last st (corner made); evenly space 91 sc along top edge; then, working into bottom of beg ch, work 3 sc in first st (corner made), *sc in each of next 2 sts, sk 1 st*, rep from * to * to last st of beg ch, work 3 sc in last st (corner made); evenly space 91 sc along bottom edge, sl st in beg sc of rnd, turn. PM for beg of rnds.

Rnd 2: Ch 1, sc in first sc, *work in established divider patt to next corner, BPdc around first sc of corner, (sc, ch 2, sc) in next sc, BPdc around 3rd sc of corner; rep from * around, sl st in first sc of rnd, turn.

Rnd 3: Ch 1, *FPdc around prev dc, sc in next sc, (sc, ch 2, sc) in ch-2 sp, sc in next sc, FPdc around prev dc, work divider patt to next corner; rep from * around, sl st to top of first dc, turn.

Rnd 4: Ch 1, sc in first sc, *work in established divider patt to next corner, BPdc around prev dc, sc in next 2 sc, (sc, ch 2, sc) in ch-2 sp, sc in next 2 sc, BPdc around next sc; rep from * around, sl st to first sc of rnd, turn.

Rnd 5: Ch 1, *FPdc around prev dc, sc in next 3 sc, (sc, ch 2, sc) in ch-2 sp, sc in next 3 sc, FPdc around prev dc, work in established divider patt to next corner; rep from * around, sl st to top of first dc, turn.

Rnd 6: Rep rnd 4, working one more sc before and after working (sc, ch 2, sc) in each corner ch-2 sp.

Fasten off. Weave in ends. Block to finished measurements using method of choice (page 11).

Striped Tote

⟫⟫ *This fabulous tote, designed by Lorna Miser, is worked in stripes of pink, purple, and off-white. You decide the color order and the width of each stripe, making your tote uniquely one of a kind. It's finished with a suede bottom and handles and is fabric lined so you can carry along your projects to work on wherever you go.*

By Lorna Miser, author of Knit Pink *(Martingale, 2013)*

SKILL LEVEL: Easy

FINISHED MEASUREMENTS:
13½" tall x 12" wide x 4" deep

FEATURED STITCHES

Chain (ch)

Double crochet (dc)

MATERIALS

Cotton Fleece from Brown Sheep Company, Inc. (80% cotton, 20% merino wool; 3.5 oz/100 g; 215 yds/197 m) ⓷

> 1 skein in color CW-240 Pink-a-Boo

> 1 skein in color CW-710 Prosperous Plum

> 1 skein in color CS-100 Cotton Ball

Serendipity Tweed from Brown Sheep Company, Inc. (60% pima cotton, 40% wool; 3.5 oz/100 g; 210 yds/191 m) ⓷

> 1 skein in color ST 64 Cherry Blossom

> 1 skein in color ST 60 Sweet Pea

Size G-6 (4 mm) crochet hook or size needed for gauge

Tapestry needle

Large suede tote bottom in color Magenta (see "Resources" on page 94)

Suede tote handles in color Magenta, 18" long (see "Resources")

Sharp yarn needle

1 yard of fabric for lining, 42" wide

1 yard Therm-O-Web HeatnBond Lite

Iron

Scissors

GAUGE

10 sts and 8 rows = 4" in patt

SPECIAL STITCH

Cluster (CL): YO, insert hook into next st, YO, pull lp through st, YO, pull through 2 lps on hook, YO, insert hook into same st, YO, pull lp through st, YO, pull through 2 lps on hook, YO, pull through rem 3 lps on hook.

PATTERN NOTES

Work 2 or 4 rows of colors randomly to keep all yarn ends on one edge so that they can easily be hidden by suede tote bottom. Lining is fused in place but could also be sewn if preferred.

TOTE

Row 1: With any color, loosely ch 34, dc in 4th ch from hook (counts as first 2 dc), work CL in each ch across, turn—30 CLs and 2 dc.

Row 2: Ch 3 (counts as first dc), dc in top of next CL, work CL in each st across to last 2 sts, CL in next dc, CL in top ch of beg ch 4 (in top of ch 3 on all subsequent rows), turn.

Rep row 2, working 2 or 4 rows of colors randomly and cutting yarn as you finish a section, leaving 6" tails, until piece measures 34".

Fasten off, but do not sew side seam. Weave in ends. Block using method of choice (page 11).

> ⫸ *You can find Lorna's knit version of the striped tote in the book* Knit Pink *(Martingale, 2013).*

FINISHING

Cut fabric lining 14" x 35". Fold one long edge down ½" for top edge of bag. Fuse Therm-O-Web to wrong side of fabric as described on label. Peel off paper backing. Align top edge of lining (folded edge) even with long side of tote that does not have the yarn ends woven into it. Align one short end. Lining should be 1" longer than remaining short end. Fuse lining to tote from the fabric side, being careful to keep all edges straight, corners square and not to fuse the overhanging lining.

Bring short ends of tote tog to close into tube. Sew tog using invisible seaming (page 10). Reaching inside tube with iron, fuse last overhanging lining in place. Insert tote into suede bottom, placing it all the way to the bottom seam of the suede, and pin in place. This overlap gives bag more structure and strength than sewing the suede to the edge of the tote. Sew using sharp yarn needle, desired yarn color, and a simple running st, going in and out of holes in suede. Pin handles in position. Sew in place using running stitch.

Abbreviations

approx	approximately	**hdc2tog**	half double crochet 2 stitches together (page 10)
beg	begin(ning)	**inc**	increase(ing)
bl	back loop	**lp(s)**	loop(s)
BPdc	back-post double crochet (page 9)	**patt**	pattern
BPtr	back-post treble crochet (page 10)	**PM**	place marker
ch	chain	**prev**	previous
ch sp	chain space	**rem**	remaining
cir	circumference	**rep**	repeat
cont	continue(ing)	**rnd(s)**	round(s)
dc	double crochet	**RS**	right side
dc2tog	double crochet 2 stitches together (page 10)	**sc**	single crochet
		sc2tog	single crochet 2 stitches together (page 10)
dcf	double crochet foundation (page 9)	**sk**	skip
dec	decrease(ing)	**sl st**	slip stitch
dtr	double treble crochet	**slst2tog**	slip stitch 2 stitches together (page 10)
esc	extended single crochet (page 8)	**sp**	space
esc2tog	extended single crochet 2 stitches together (page 10)	**st(s)**	stitch(es)
fl	front loop	**tog**	together
FPdc	front-post double crochet (page 9)	**tr**	treble crochet
FPtr	front-post treble crochet (page 10)	**WS**	wrong side
hdc	half double crochet	**YO**	yarn over
hdcf	half double crochet foundation (page 9)		

Cancer Awareness Colors

You may choose to crochet any of these designs in a different color of hope. This list of colors is from ChooseHope.com.

All cancer survivors	Lavender
Bladder cancer	Marigold/blue/purple
Brain cancer	Gray
Breast cancer	Pink
Childhood cancer	Gold
Colon cancer	Dark blue
Esophageal cancer	Periwinkle blue
Head and neck cancer	Burgundy/ivory
Hodgkin's lymphoma	Violet
Kidney cancer	Orange
Leiomyosarcoma	Purple
Leukemia	Orange
Lung cancer	White
Lymphoma	Lime Green
Melanoma	Black
Multiple myeloma	Burgundy
Ovarian cancer	Teal
Pancreatic cancer	Purple
Prostate cancer	Light blue
Testicular cancer	Orchid
Thyroid cancer	Teal/pink/blue
Uterine cancer	Peach

Helpful Information

YARN WEIGHTS						
Yarn- Weight Symbol and Category Name	**(1)** Super Fine	**(2)** Fine	**(3)** Light	**(4)** Medium	**(5)** Bulky	**(6)** Super Bulky
Types of Yarn in Category	Sock, Fingering, Baby	Sport, Baby	DK, Light Worsted	Worsted, Afghan, Aran	Chunky, Craft, Rug	Bulky, Roving
Crochet Gauge Ranges* in Single Crochet to 4"	21 to 32 sts	16 to 20 sts	12 to 17 sts	11 to 14 sts	8 to 11sts	5 to 9 sts
Recommended Hook in Metric Size Range	2.25 to 3.5 mm	3.5 to 4.5 mm	4.5 to 5.5 mm	5.5 to 6.5 mm	6.5 to 9 mm	9 mm and larger
Recommended Hook in US Size Range	B-1 to E-4	E-4 to 7	7 to I-9	I-9 to K-10½	K-10½ to M-13	M-13 and larger

These are guidelines only. The above reflect the most commonly used gauges and needle or hook sizes for specific yarn categories.

CROCHET HOOK SIZES

Millimeter	US Size*
2.25 mm	B-1
2.75 mm	C-2
3.25 mm	D-3
3.5 mm	E-4
3.75 mm	F-5
4 mm	G-6
4.5 mm	7
5 mm	H-8
5.5 mm	I-9
6 mm	J-10
6.5 mm	K-10½
8 mm	L-11
9 mm	M/N-13
10 mm	N/P-15

Letter or number may vary. Rely on the millimeter sizing.

STEEL HOOK SIZES

Millimeter	US Size*
2.75 mm	1
2.25 mm	2
1.65 mm	7

METRIC CONVERSIONS

Yards x .91 = meters

Meters x 1.09 = yards

Ounces x 28.35 = grams

Grams x .035 = ounces

SKILL LEVELS

Beginner: Projects for first-time crocheters using basic stitches; minimal shaping.

Easy: Projects using yarn with basic stitches, repetitive stitch patterns, simple color changes, and simple shaping and finishing.

Intermediate: Projects using a variety of techniques, such as basic lace patterns or color patterns; midlevel shaping and finishing.

Experienced: Projects with intricate stitch patterns, techniques, and dimension, such as non-repeating patterns, multicolor techniques, fine threads, small hooks, detailed shaping, and refined finishing.

Resources

Contact the following companies to find shops that carry the yarns featured in this book.

Berroco
berroco.com
Comfort DK

Blue Sky Alpacas
blueskyalpacas.com
Suri Merino
Brushed Suri

Brown Sheep Company, Inc.
brownsheep.com
Cotton Fleece
Lamb's Pride Worsted
Lanaloft Worsted
Serendipity Tweed
Wildfoote Luxury Sock

Classic Elite Yarns
classiceliteyarns.com
Silky Alpaca Lace

Cascade Yarns
cascadeyarns.com
Cascade 220
Kid Seta

Coats and Clark
coatsandclark.com
Fashion by Aunt Lydia's Crochet Thread
Classic 10 by Aunt Lydia's Crochet Thread

Hidden Valley Farm and Woolen Mill
hiddenvalleyfarmwoolenmill.com
Birch

Interlacements
interlacementsyarns.com
Irish Linen

Jojoland
jojoland.com
Cashmere Lace Weight
Tonic

Juniper Moon Farm
fiberfarm.com
Findley

Knit Picks
knitpicks.com
Capra DK
Shine Sport

Knitting Fever
knittingfever.com
Baby Joey's Baby Silk by Queensland Collection
Mulberry by Louisa Harding

Lion Brand Yarn
lionbrand.com
Nature's Choice Organic Cotton
Superwash Merino Cashmere

Lorna's Laces
lornaslaces.net
Shepherd Sock (part of the proceeds for the color Flamingo Pink go to charity)

Plymouth Yarn Company Inc.
plymouthyarn.com
Worsted Merino Superwash

Patons
patonsyarns.com
Divine
Lace

Skacel Collection, Inc.
skacelknitting.com
CoBaSi by HiKoo

Somerset Designs
somersetdesigns.com
Suede tote bottom and suede handles

Acknowledgments

From concept to final product, it takes a great many people contributing all manner of talents to bring a book to fruition. To everyone at Martingale, my heartfelt thanks for the hard work and dedication given to bringing *Crochet Pink* to the bookshelves. You are a great group of people to work with.

Although it's impossible to list everyone, there are a few people I would like to acknowledge, with appreciation for their support and contributions.

Karen Costello Soltys, managing editor. Thank you for the opportunity to write *Crochet Pink*. It's a book I've wanted to do for a very long time and a cause very close to my heart. I truly did enjoy this project.

Cathy Reitan, author liaison. Thank you for all your help and support.

Ursula Reikes, technical editor. It was so great to be able to work with you again. Your suggestions and corrections make me look so good. Thank you so much for all your attention to detail and for keeping me on track.

Carol Lykins, Bee Hahn, Michelle Zahn, and Sharon Blosch, model makers. I can't thank you enough for all your hard work in not only crocheting models for me, but also for your helpful suggestions in making many of my instructions clearer. Have I told you all that you totally rock?!

Cheryl Fall and Kathryn Conway, illustrators. Thank you for the wonderful illustrations. Your work makes my instructions easier to follow.

Harrison Richards, Furls Crochet Hooks. I can't believe you made me a pink crochet hook! It's beautiful and I can't thank you enough for providing such a wonderful item for my book.

Michelle Zahn, the Soap Lady. You made me hearts! Perfect soap hearts in pink and white! Thank you, Michelle.

Contributing Designers

I want to thank some wonderful people for contributing their talents to this project and providing some great designs.

Lorna Miser took up knitting in 1983 when her first child was born. Within a short time she was spinning and dyeing her own yarns and started Lorna's Laces. By 2003, Lorna's Laces had grown in size and popularity and she sold the company. Since then Lorna has pursued her designing, writing, and teaching career in the yarn industry. *Knit Pink* (Martingale, 2013), a companion book to this one, is Lorna's fourth published book.

Rozetta (Bee) Hahn owns her business as a therapeutic massage therapist. She is also a fabulous knitter, spinner, and crocheter. Her designs have won several ribbons and awards, including best in show. Bee and I have worked together on several creations and I'm very happy to have her contributions to this book as designer, model maker, and huge shoulder to lean on. Thanks, Bee, for everything!

Carol Lykins, my sister, has been crocheting since she was taught at a young age by our grandmother. She works with me and Knitted Threads Designs, LLC, as a contract model maker and pattern proofer. Not only have we codesigned many projects over the years, but Carol's own designs have appeared in several Martingale publications. Oh, yes, and have I told you what a wonderful sister you are, Carol? Without your help, I would have floundered.